BETRAYAL OF DUE PROCESS

A Comparative Assessment of Plea Bargaining in the United States and Canada

Hedieh Nasheri

University Press of America,® Inc.
Lanham • New York • Oxford

University Press of America,® Inc.
4720 Boston Way
Lanham, Maryland 20706

12 Hid's Copse Rd.
Cumnor Hill, Oxford OX2 9JJ

Printed in the United States of America
British Library Cataloging in Publication Information Available

Library of Congress Cataloging-in-Publication Data

Nasheri, Hedieh.
Betrayal of due process : a comparative assessment of plea bargaining in the United States and Canada / Hedieh Nasheri.
p. cm..
Includes bibliographical references and index.
1. Plea bargaining—United States. 2. Plea bargaining—United States—History. 3. Plea bargaining—Canada. 4. Plea bargaining—Canada—History. I. Title.
KDZ972.N34 1998 347.73'72—dc21 98-16031 CIP

ISBN 0-7618-1108-7 (cloth: alk. ppr.)
ISBN 0-7618-1109-5 (pbk: alk. ppr.)

™ The paper used in this publication meets the minimum requirements of American National Standard for Information Sciences—Permanence of Paper for Printed Library Materials, ANSI Z39.48—1984

To
Timothy J. O'Hearn
My Best Friend

COMMENTS OF REVIEWERS

This is an excellent comparative analysis of plea bargaining. Nasheri's approach is multidisciplinary in that she uses historical, case law and comparative methods to weave description and critical analysis into a coherent and insightful study of the practice of plea bargaining in the United States and Canada. This book is a significant contribution to the emerging field of comparative criminal justice.

Professor John A. Conley, Dean
School of Social and Behavioral Sciences
California State University

Betrayal of Due Process is a clearly written book on a very important topic. Nasheri's ability to integrate system descriptions with comparative analysis makes it both an excellent example of what comparative criminal justice research should accomplish, and a useful source of practical information.

Professor Philip L. Reichel
Director of Criminal Justice Studies
University of Northern Colorado

Hedieh Nasheri's "Betrayal of Due Process" provides an in-depth account of the development of the plea bargaining process in two distinct legal systems, Canada and the United States. It stands as an ideal elaboration of Packer's "due process model", showing how justice systems seek to limit or expand civil rights through the use of discretion.
Nasheri's analysis also provides a framework for the study of social control by showing how the objectives of punishment are shaped by the individual-level tactics employed within justice systems.

Professor Larry Siegel
Department of Criminal Justice
University of Massachusetts

CONTENTS

Contents

PREFACE

This book presents a comparative analysis of the ideological and historical development of the practice of plea bargaining in the United States and Canada. This book grew out of personal observations and discussions I had while executing a research grant provided by the Canadian Government. In the course of that research, I became interested in similarities between the United States and Canadian criminal justice systems. In particular, I became interested in the differences between the philosophical rhetoric of each system and my observations of their day-to-day operations in the behind-the-scenes practice of plea bargaining or plea negotiation.

The book is designed primarily to provide a detailed historical and legal review of the justification and circumstances surrounding plea bargaining practices in these countries. In addition, the book borrows the landmark theoretical framework of Packer to develop the discussion, but only as a point of reference. This work is not intended to be a theoretical sociological analysis of cause and effect. It also is not meant to test or explore Packer's conceptual framework of due process and crime control. Rather, Packer is used only as a point of reference.

The book focuses on the practice of plea bargaining from the late 1920s to the present time. Special attention is given to recent decades when the High Courts in both countries first gave close attention to this practice. Issues such as differences in theoretical justifications, differences in definitions, differences in the day-to-day practices, and differences in the present status of the practice are examined.

There is no published historical comparative analysis of this aspect of the criminal justice system between these neighboring countries, and little has been written on the origins of plea bargaining. According to Lawrence Friedman, who has studied the history of plea bargaining, "the history of plea bargaining is [a] fairly blank chapter in the history of criminal justice."

This book is not easily categorized since it cuts across several academic disciplines. There are no books that I know of involving a cross-national comparison of plea negotiation practices. This book presents a legal, historical analysis of the development and perception of plea bargaining activities among those involved in the practice, rather than an abstract model attempting to explain or analyze such social phenomena.

Plea bargaining has long been an integral part of the administration of justice. It was practiced for many years-- but not acknowledged or discussed in public -- and only in recent decades has the public been made well-aware of its existence. As plea bargaining has become a major institution in both the United States and Canada, a comparative study of the reactions to it is useful to explore how the lawmakers of these nations have justified this practice and to explore whether it is being or can be successfully used to achieve case resolutions that are as equitable to the state and to the defendant as a jury trial.

ACKNOWLEDGMENT

This book was made possible by many individuals. Without their help and encouragement I would have been far too overwhelmed (not to mention enormously depressed) to finish it. I am particularly grateful to members of the judiciary and the Bar in Cuyahoga County, Ohio and in Ontario Province, Canada. Thanks to all the people listed below for their assistance, their time, feedback and suggestions which made the preparation of this book possible. Justice Arthur G. Martin, Justice Marc Rosenberg, the Honorable Michael Dambrot, the Honorable Frank Gorman, the Honorable Paul J. LeSage and Justice Cou, George Sadd, Edward Galler, Sarah Welch, Michael Innes, Alan Rossman, Richard W. Pogue, George J. Moscarino, Hyman Friedman, members of the Canadian and the American Bar Associations, members of the Cuyahoga County Prosecutor Office and the Public Defenders Office, members of the Cuyahoga County Common Pleas Court, and members of the Ontario Ministry of the Attorney General & the Provincial Crown Attorney Office. Very sincere thanks is expressed to the Canadian Embassy for providing a research grant for research in Canada. I also would like to thank the librarians for their research assistant at the Ontario Archives, Osgoode Society of Upper Canada, University of Toronto Law Library, York University Law Library, Case Western Reserve Law Library, Cuyahoga County Law Library, the Historical Society , and the Cleveland Public Library. I have benefited from the helpful comments and suggestions received from a number of faculty at the Case Western Reserve University School of Law and the faculty of the Social Policy History Department. Thanks is also due to the reviewers for their insight and honesty. I am indebted to Timothy J. O'Hearn for his time, talents, expertise and his contribution to the preparation of this book. Finally, I would like to thank members of my family, my mother & father and my husband for their moral and emotional support which made the publication of this book possible.

CHAPTER 1
INTRODUCTION

"The law embodies the story of a nation's development through the centuries . . . ."[1]

This book presents a comparison of plea bargaining[2] practices in the United States and Canada. The book provides an interpretive and historical review of plea bargaining practices and of the rationales behind them. The book is not intended to propose a sociological theory or model to explain the practice or to predict its future. Rather, the book proceeds from the premise that the examination of this common method for resolving criminal cases[3] provides insights into the fundamental differences and similarities between American and Canadian practices in the administration of criminal justice.

SIMILARITIES AND DIFFERENCES

Many Americans appear to view all of North America as a single homogeneous society. Robin Winks explains this well in his book, *The Relevance of Canadian History*, where he describes an American view "[t]hat Canadians are basically like Americans [but] . . . Canadians have a monarchical and parliamentary system of government." He explains that many Americans do not see a difference between their experience and the Canadian experience.[4] Similarly, Richard Lipsey, a Canadian professor, observed that, while most well-informed Canadians know a great deal about the United States, the reverse cannot be said about most well-informed Americans.[5] According to Lipsey, this was confirmed beyond doubt by

Willis C. Armstrong of the United States embassy in Ottawa who wrote in 1976: "The American public is conscious of the fact that there are intergovernmental relations, but sometimes wonders why there is an American embassy in Ottawa, because it is not clear to them that Canada is a country, let alone a foreign country."[6]

Of course, many criticize such a simplistic view. As Mr. Armstrong wrote: "Ignorance of this basic fact [that Canada is different than America], coupled with American unawareness of the striving of Canadian elites for some identifiable set of qualities to distinguish Canada from the United States, can lead to misunderstanding."[7] Professor Seymour Martin Lipset also notes the differences between the two countries, pointing out that: "[A]lthough these new peoples [America and Canada] probably resemble each other more than any other two nations on earth, there are consistent patterns of difference between them."[8]

The differences between the United States and Canada are discussed at length in Lipset's book, *The First New Nation: The United States in Historical and Comparative Perspective*, published in 1963,[9] and in his essay "Canada and the United States: The Cultural Dimension" published in 1985. Lipset observes that Canada has been a more conservative, traditional, law-abiding, status conscious and elitist society than the United States. He further observes that, although both differ from the post-feudal European nations, Canada has remained more like traditional Britain and France than has the United States.[10] The variations between Canada and the United States stem from the founding event which gave birth to both, that is, the American Revolution, and from variations in their political and legal institutions.[11] Similarly, W.L. Morton's work in 1961, *The Canadian Identity*, emphasizes that Canada "arrived at freedom through evolution in allegiance and not by revolutionary compact. Hence, her final governing force . . . is tradition and convention."[12]

One would expect that the differences and similarities between the United States and Canada would be reflected in the major institutions of those societies, such as their criminal justice systems. The American and Canadian criminal justice systems do not function apart from the societies they serve. Rather, they mirror each society and influence the lives of their citizens.

A fundamental concept of both United States and Canadian jurisprudence provides that justice is best achieved through an adversarial process which, according to certain rules, receives evidence, makes findings of fact, and applies the law. Nonetheless, the shortcut of plea bargaining has developed into a widely used vehicle for dispensing justice in both countries.

Consequently, plea bargaining is an important facet of the criminal justice systems of both countries which cannot be ignored in any meaningful comparative study.

A Point Of Reference

This book uses a theoretical framework borrowed from Herbert Packer to aid the discussion. In Herbert Packer's landmark book, *The Limits of the Criminal Sanction*, Packer articulates two paradigms of criminal justice processes. These concepts represent separate value systems that compete for priority in the operation of any criminal justice process. The purpose of using Packer's conceptual models in this book is to provide a point of reference and to enhance the comparative analysis. It is not the purpose of this book to test Packer's model or to develop another sociological model to replace it.

The first of Packer's paradigms is called the "crime control model." The value system that underlies the crime control model "is based on the proposition that the repression of criminal conduct is by far the most important function to be performed by the criminal justice process."[13] Failure to bring criminal conduct under proper control is viewed as leading to the breakdown of public order, and hence the disappearance of an important condition of human freedom. Accordingly, the ultimate objective is that the criminal justice process be a positive guarantor of social freedom.

In order to achieve this purpose, systems that follow the "crime control model" require that primary attention be paid to the efficiency with which the criminal justice process operates to screen suspects, determine guilt and secure appropriate disposition of persons convicted of crime.[14] The efficiency of the system refers to the system's capacity to apprehend, try, convict and dispose of a high proportion of criminal offenders whose offenses become known. As such, there is a premium on speed and finality. Speed in turn depends on informality and on uniformity. Finality depends on minimizing the occasions for challenge. The process must not be cluttered with ceremonies or rituals that do not advance the disposition of the case. By the application of administrative expertise, primarily that of the police and prosecutors, an early determination of the probability of innocence or guilt emerges. Those who are probably innocent are screened out. Those who are probably guilty are passed quickly through the remaining stages of the process.

The key feature of the model, which applies to those who are not screened out, is what Packer calls a "presumption of guilt."[15] The presumption of guilt is purely and simply a prediction of outcome that begins to operate well before a "suspect" becomes a "defendant." The "presumption of guilt" found in Packer's "crime control model" is not simply the opposite of the "presumption of innocence" found in the "due process model." The two concepts are uniquely different ideas rather than opposite ideas. The presumption of innocence means that, until there has been an adjudication of guilt by a proper legal authority, the suspect is to be treated as if his guilt is an open question, for reasons other than the probable outcome of the case. Thus, while the presumption of innocence is normative and not a prediction of outcome, the presumption of guilt is a descriptive and a factual prediction of outcome.

The "presumption of guilt" provides the crime control model with a basis for accepting that the dominant goal of repressing crime can be achieved through a highly summary process without any great loss of efficiency. Indeed, the model takes an even stronger position -- that subsequent process steps, particularly those of a formal adjudicatory nature, are unlikely to determine facts as reliably as the expert administrative process steps that precede them.

Thus, in the "crime control model" the emphasis lies in early administrative fact-finding stages. The subsequent stages are relatively unimportant and should be truncated as much as possible. The crime control model, when reduced to its barest essentials and operating at maximum efficiency, offers two optimum results from the administrative fact-finding process: (1) exoneration of the suspect, or (2) the entry of a guilty plea.

Packer's second and opposing paradigm is the "due process" model. The value system that underlies the due process model is composed of a mixture of ideas, some of them based on judgments about the efficacy of crime control devices, others having to do with quite different considerations. As a result, the "due process model" looks very much like an obstacle course.

The ideology of due process manifests itself upon the formal structure of law more so than the ideology of crime control. It focuses on exclusionary rules of evidence, the right to counsel, and other procedural safeguards.[16] The "crime control" model places heavy reliance on the ability of investigative and prosecutorial officers to reconstruct an accurate account of what actually took place in an alleged criminal act. By contrast, the due process model rejects this premise and assumes, instead, that the existence of an informal, non-adjudicative fact-finding process provides significant possibility of error.[17] While there are many obstacles in seeking justice, the primary objective of the due process model, according to some, is "finding the truth."[18]

There are various arguments in favor of the due process model. For example, people are notoriously poor observers of disturbing events.[19] The more emotion that is connected with an incident, the greater the possibility that recollection will be incorrect.[20] Witnesses may be motivated by bias or interest which may go uncovered by government officials, such as the police. Considerations such as these lead to a rejection of informal fact-finding processes as a definitive arbiter of factual guilt, and result in formal, adversarial fact-finding processes.

Even then, however, the distrust of fact-finding processes that lie at the core of the due process model is not satisfied. Because of the ongoing possibilities of human error, further scrutiny is necessary, or, at the least, must be available in case facts are overlooked or suppressed in the heat of battle.[21] With this framework, the "due process model" "resembles a factory devoting a substantial part of its input to quality control."[22] As a consequence, the focus on quality control cuts down on the quantitative output.

The most obvious and potentially far-reaching mechanism by which the "due process model" implements these anti-authoritarian values is the standard for proving legal guilt. Under this model, a person may not be held guilty for a crime merely on a showing that, based upon reliable evidence, he or she probably did what he or she is said to have done. Instead, the person is to be held guilty if, and only if, these factual determinations are made in a procedurally regular fashion and by authorities acting within competence duly allocated to them.[23] Furthermore, the person may not be held guilty, even though the factual determination is adverse to him or her, if various rules designed to protect the person and to safeguard the integrity of the process were compromised. As such, the tribunal that convicts this person must have the power to deal with this case ("jurisdiction"); the case must be held in a geographically appropriate place ("venue"); too long a time must not have elapsed since the person was accused of the crime ("statute of limitations"); the accused must not have been previously charged with the same or substantially similar offense for the same actions ("double jeopardy"); the accused must not fall within a category of persons, such as children or the insane, who are legally immune from conviction ("criminal responsibility"); and so on. None of these requirements deal with the factual question of whether the person did or did not engage in the conduct charged. Yet favorable answers to any of these questions will result in the accused being pronounced legally innocent.

Two Canadian researchers, John Hagan and Jeffrey Leon, have compared several aspects of the American and Canadian legal systems, applying

Packer's "due process" and "crime control" paradigms. They explain that the notion of due process is based, in part, on John Locke's Enlightenment theory that the law should be used effectively in defense of "natural" and "inalienable rights."[24] The crime control model is typical of Edmund Burke's conservative reaction to the Enlightenment, which contends that civil liberties can have meaning only in an orderly society. Hagan and Leon note that the distinction between these models is one of degree, and assert that Canadians tend toward the crime control model, while Americans stress due process:

> The due process model is much concerned with exclusionary rules of evidence, the right to counsel, and other procedural safeguards thought useful in protecting accused persons from unjust applications of criminal sanctions.
>
> . . . The crime control model places heavy emphasis on the repression of criminal conduct, arguing that only by insuring order can individuals in a society be guaranteed personal freedom. It is for this reason that advocates of crime control are less anxious to protect such persons against sometimes dubious findings of guilt.[25]

They further observe:

> There is a very persistent and significant difference in Canadian and American attitudes toward issues of due process and crime control. This difference is that Canadians are more willing than Americans to forego law reforms in favor of leaving to legal authorities the discretion to decide what accused and convicted persons require and deserve. This difference in attitude and practice, with the Canadian emphasis on ensuring fairness to the accused rather than on a strict adherence to inalienable rights [is shown repeatedly in court decisions].[26]

These observations about the criminal justice system of the United States and Canada will be revisited later in this book and examined in light of the practice of plea bargaining.

The Focus Of This Book

This book presents a comparative analysis of the ideological and historical development of the practice of plea bargaining in the United States and

Canada. One of the values of intellectual and legal-historical analysis is to gain perspective on our own place and time.

The focus of this work is primarily on the practice of plea bargaining from the late 1920s (when public concern over it seems to have been widespread) to the present time (when it is accepted as routine). Special attention is given to recent decades (1960s and 1970s) when the High Courts in both countries paid increased attention to this practice. Issues such as differences and similarities in underlying theory, definitions, in the day-to-day practices, in public concern and concern among legal practitioners, and in the present status of the practice are examined thoroughly. These comparisons are further explored by analyzing landmark cases in both countries. As explained in later chapters, the expedient of plea bargaining has been part of legal procedure in the United States and Canada since the mid-nineteenth century. For this reason, these earlier periods are also examined.

There is no historical comparative analysis of this aspect of the criminal justice system between these neighboring countries, and little has been written on the origins of plea bargaining. As one scholar stated, "the history of plea bargaining is [a] fairly blank chapter in the history of criminal justice."[27] A comparison of the practice of plea bargaining in the United States and Canada in this century, and a comparison of theoretical justifications articulated for the practice during those years, reveals significant differences between these nations considering their common origins in Anglo-Saxon criminal law.

This book will consider whether a comparison of the practice of plea bargaining in the United States and Canada in recent decades supports the "crime control" versus "due process" tendencies of Canada and the United States observed by Hagan and Leon. As plea bargaining has become a major institution in both the United States and Canada, a comparative study of the intellectual reaction to it is necessary to explore how the lawmakers of these nations have justified this practice and to explore whether it is being, or can be, successfully used to achieve case resolutions that are as equitable to the state and to the defendant as a jury trial would be. As Lipset very eloquently has pointed out "a complex society is under constant pressure to adjust its institutions to its central value system. Thus the value system of a society influences the character of its institutions and these shape the character of its citizens as they grow up. The character of a society's members in turn reacts upon the character of its institutions".[28]

RESEARCH METHODOLOGY

Two jurisdictions were selected for this analysis -- the State of Ohio, as exemplified by the criminal justice system of its most populous county, Cuyahoga County; and Ontario Province, as seen in dominion and provincial courts in Toronto. The book is based upon extensive research in the published works of the legal profession, of legal historians and of social scientists, as well as a review of primary and secondary materials.[29] This book also is based upon personal observations by the author, gained from observing numerous pretrials and plea discussions. These were attended in the United States and Canada while working pursuant to a Canadian Government Research grant in the Public Defender's office of Cuyahoga County and at the Provincial Crown Attorney's office in Ontario. In addition, interviews were conducted with judges, prosecutors, defense attorneys and court administrators at the dominion and provincial levels in Toronto, and with county prosecutors, attorneys and judges in Cleveland. The interview sessions involved extensive questions regarding the plea bargaining practice in both jurisdictions.

NOTES

1. Oliver Wendell Holmes, The Common Law Lecture (1881), I.
2. Plea bargaining is the process by which the defendant in a criminal case relinquishes his right to go to trial in exchange for a reduction in charge and/or sentence. It is a bargain consisting of the exchange of official concessions for the defendant's act of self-conviction. Plea bargaining may resolve by (1) sentence recommendation; (2) the plea to a lesser included offense; or (3) dismissal of charges in an indictment, information, or other charging paper. "Plea bargaining" is a term for a practice that has also been referred to by various other names such as "plea negotiations," "compromise of criminal cases," "plea discussion" and "plea argument." Yale Kamisar, Wayne LaFave, and Jerold Israel, *Modern Criminal Procedure* (St. Paul, Minn.: West Publishing Company, 1995). *See also* Albert W. Alschuler, "Plea Bargaining and its History," *Law and Society Review* 13 (1979): 213. *See also* A. D. Klein, "Plea Bargaining," *Criminal Law Quarterly* 14 (1971-72): 289.
3. Abraham S. Blumberg, "The Practice of Law as a Confidence Game: Organizational Co-Optation of a Profession," *Law and Society Review* 1 (1967): 18. "The overwhelming majority of convictions in criminal cases (usually over 90%) are not the product of a combative trial-by-jury process, but instead merely the sentencing of the individual after a negotiated, bargained-for plea of guilty has been entered." Ibid. *See also* Brian A. Grosman, *The Prosecutor: An Inquiry into Exercise of Discretion* (Toronto: University of Toronto Press, 1969), 41.

4. *See* Robin Winks, *The Relevance of Canadian History: United States and Imperial Perspective* (Toronto: The Macmillan Company of Canada Limited, 1979).

5. Richard G. Lipsey, "Canada and the United States: The Economic Dimension," in *Canada and the United States: Enduring Friendship, Persistent Stress*, ed. Charles S. Doran and John S. Siegler, (Englewood Cliffs, N.J.: Prentice-Hall, 1985), 69-70.

6. Ibid.

7. Ibid.

8. Lipsey, "The Economic Dimension," 69-70. *See also* Seymour Martin Lipset, "Canada and the United States: The Cultural Dimension," in *Canada and the United States: Enduring Friendship, Persistent Stress*, ed. Charles S. Doran and John S. Siegler (Englewood Cliffs, N.J.: Prentice-Hall, 1985).

9. *See* Seymour Martin Lipset, *The First New Nation: The United States in Historical and Comparative Perspective* (New York: New York Basic Books, 1963).

10. Lipset, "The Cultural Dimension," 110.

11. Ibid.

12. Ibid., 113.

13. Herbert Packer, *The Limits of the Criminal Sanction* (Stanford, Calif.: Stanford University Press, 1968), 158.

14. *See* Lloyd E. Ohlin, "Surveying Discretion by Criminal Justice Decision Makers," in *Discretion in Criminal Justice: The Tension Between Individualization and Uniformity*, ed. Lloyd E. Ohlin and Frank J. Remington (Albany, N.Y.: State University of New York Press, 1993), 10-11.

15. Packer, *Criminal Sanction*, 160.

16. Carol R. Goforth, "A Jurisprudential Reflection upon the Burger Court's Approach to Procedural Due Process," *Arkansas Law Review* 42 (1989): 838-840, 852-853, 861-862, 869. *See also* Benjamin E. Rosenberg, "Rethinking the Right to Due Process in Connection With Pretrial Identification Procedures: An Analysis and a Proposal," *Kentucky Law Journal* 79 (1990-91): 290-295.

17. Packer, *Criminal Sanction*, 163.

18. David A. Harris, "The Constitution and Truth Seeking: A New Theory On Expert Services for Indigent Defendants," *The Journal of Criminal Law & Criminology* 83 (1992): 494.

19. Packer, *Criminal Sanction*, 158.

20. Harris, "The Constitution and Truth Seeking," 494.

21. *See* Robert M. Bloom, "Judicial Integrity: A Call for its Re-emergence in the Adjudication of Criminal Cases," *The Journal of Criminal Law & Criminology* 84 (1993): 478-482.

22. Packer, *Criminal Sanction*, 165.

23. Donald A. Dripps, "At the Borders of the Fourth Amendment: Why a Real Due Process Test Should Replace the Outrageous Government Conduct Defense," *University of Illinois Law Review* 2 (1993): 261-262, 277-278.

24. *See* Wilfried Bottke, "'Rule of Law' or 'Due Process' as a Common Feature of Criminal Process in Western Democratic Societies," *University of Pittsburgh Law Review* 51 (1990): 419, 456.

25. Packer, *Criminal Sanction*, 129.

26. John Hagan and Jeffrey Leon, "The Rehabilitation of Law: A Social-Historical Comparison of Probation in Canada and the United States," *Canadian Journal of Sociology* 5 (1980): 235, 248.

27. Lawrence M. Friedman, "Plea Bargaining in Historical Perspective," *Law and Society Review* 7 (1979): 247-259.

28. Lipset, *The First New Nation* (1963).

29. In Canada, this included review of Attorney General's Series, files, criminal and civil; circular letters to Crown attorneys; 1993 Ontario A.G. Report; other correspondence and memos from the Province of Ontario at the Ontario Archives; review of Supreme Court, court of appeals cases and other criminal cases; the Oral History Collection of the Osgood Society of Upper Canada held at the Ontario Archives in Toronto; reports on administration of Ontario courts, Law Society of Upper Canada; Special Lectures 1969 "Panel Discussion, Law Reform Commission of Canada"; criminal procedure; working papers of the Law Society of Upper Canada; Canadian Bar Association records; and the Legislative Assembly press clippings. It also included, in the United States, a review of: *The Cleveland Foundation Survey of Criminal Justice in Cleveland, Part I: Criminal Courts* by Reginal Heber Smith and Herbert B. Ehrmann and *Part II: Prosecution* by Alfred Bettman; an outline of the Cleveland Crime Survey by Raymond Moley; monthly *Cleveland Crime Commission Bulletin*; *Ohio Bar Journals*; *Encyclopedia of Cleveland History*; *American Bar Association Journal*; American Bar Foundation Research Journal; ABA, "Standard for Criminal Justice," National Advisory Commission on Criminal Justice, "Standards and Goals"; court reports, President's Commission on Law Enforcement and Criminal Justice; review of Supreme Court, court of appeals cases and other criminal cases; and various Law Review articles.

CHAPTER 2

THE WELL-ESTABLISHED AND WELL-ACCEPTED PRACTICE IN THE UNITED STATES

The practice of plea bargaining is well institutionalized in the United States. It operates quickly and efficiently. But it is debatable whether the prevailing practice adequately protects constitutional rights and achieves "justice" in accordance with the concept of due process, or whether it is a routine procedure with a life of its own, divorced from historical concepts of due process.

GENERAL BACKGROUND: THE ROLE OF THE ACTORS

To understand the reality of plea bargaining, the roles of the participants must be understood, with particular attention to the motivations for engaging in plea negotiations. The practices of these participants will be examined in order to consider their relationship to the concept of due process.

THE ROLE OF THE PROSECUTOR

Before the prosecutor becomes involved in a case, there must be an arrest by police officers who take an accused into custody and charge him or her with the commission of a crime. Initially, the determination of charging the accused is made either through a preliminary hearing, where a magistrate reviews the prosecution's case in open court, or through a private grand jury proceeding. The defendant is then supposed to be given fair notice of the criminal charges and an opportunity to contest them. Thereafter, pre-trial procedures takes place, which varies depending on whether the defendant is charged with a misdemeanor (a minor crime for which the penalty is usually less than one year in jail, or a fine), or a felony (a serious crime generally punishable by one year or more in prison). The pre-trial procedure is a crucial stage in the process, in that it often determines the outcome of the case.

The pre-trial process starts with the initial appearance (arraignment). The accused is formally apprised of the charges and the judge or magistrate determines whether the defendant is entitled to some form of pre-trial release, often with the posting of bail, or must remain in custody. The judge or magistrate also determines whether it is necessary to appoint counsel, which is provided by the state, to represent the accused. Eventually, there is a plea of guilty or not guilty.

THE ROLE OF THE DEFENSE ATTORNEY OR PUBLIC DEFENDER

At the initial stage of a criminal prosecution in the United States, after the defendant has been charged by a magistrate or a grand jury proceeding, the accused obtains his own defense lawyer or the state provides one for him, depending on his financial status. In Cuyahoga County, the arraignment room in the felony division is controlled by a judge. Every two weeks a new judge is placed in the arraignment room. Each judge has his or her own approach as to how many cases to give to the public defender's office, and how many cases to assign through the private bar when the defendant cannot obtain his or her own defense attorney. On average, the county public defender's office assumes approximately one-third of the docket for the year.[1]

The defendant is required to appear at an arraignment (initial appearance), where she pleads guilty or not guilty to the charges. If the accused pleads guilty, obviously there will be no trial. If the accused does not plead guilty, then until the time of trial, plea bargaining can take place. The defense attorney at the arraignment consults his client, and thereafter may approach the prosecutor for some concession, usually consisting of a reduction in the number or seriousness of the charges. The defendant, upon pleading guilty, may thereby negotiate to lessen the degree of his potential punishment. If he pleads not guilty, then a trial is scheduled.

After the arraignment, the defense attorney or the public defender may file motions with the court prior to trial. Typical pre-trial motions include motions to dismiss; motions to determine the competency of a defendant to stand trial; motions to suppress illegally obtained evidence; motions to suppress a pre-trial identification of the accused; motions to require the prosecution to disclose the identity of a confidential informant; motions to change venue (location) of the trial; or motions to obtain a continuance (postponement) of the trial.

Prior to trial, there also will be pre-trial discovery. The prosecutor is obliged to disclose exculpatory evidence (i.e., evidence tending to vindicate the accused). The defense attorney also is required to disclose evidence to the prosecutor in accordance with certain procedural rules.[2] A Cuyahoga County public defender explained the pre-trial discovery process as follows:

> Prosecutors read from police reports, to tell you what the case is, giving you an idea of who witnesses are, statements the clients made and regularly won't give you exculpatory evidence . . . They read from a police report, of what questions will be made from it for trial . . . [sometimes] you don't get discovery until filing of motions. . . .[3]

THE ROLE OF THE JUDGE

The trial judge first becomes involved in a pre-trial conference where all parties (defense attorney and the prosecutor) meet with the judge, in the absence of the defendant, to discuss the case. If the defendant has agreed to plead guilty, the judge will take his plea under consideration and usually the prosecutor, based on a prior agreement with defendant and his counsel, will recommend a sentence to the judge. In most cases, the judge accepts the recommended sentence.

Before a defendant can plead guilty, however, the judge is required to make the defendant aware of the elements of the offense in order to ensure that the accused will not mistakenly admit guilt. The judge also must apprise the defendant of his constitutional alternatives to pleading guilty. The judge informs the defendant of all reasonably foreseeable consequences of conviction in order to respect the defendant's right to choose.[4]

If the accused proceeds to trial and is convicted of a crime, the judge must impose a sentence. The judge can choose among a variety of punishments, including probation, community service, community control, monetary fines, incarceration, or death.

While the preceding summary merely outlines common procedures that every accused person goes through, in reality, much more occurs at each stage of the criminal justice process, both on and off the record. In the criminal justice arena, it is important to remember that the reality does not consist solely of the fine points of law found in appellate court opinions. The reality of law is found in the actions of individual police officers on the street, prosecutors and defense attorneys in pre-trial proceedings, and only occasionally in actual criminal trials. These less formal stages of criminal process are what Yale Kamisar once called the 'gatehouses' of American criminal procedure. Although largely hidden from public view, they are far more important in terms of the actual input on people's lives than the more visible 'mansions' represented by the opinions of appellate court judges.[5]

Rules And Regulations Governing Plea Bargaining

PROCEDURAL RULES AND THE ABA STANDARDS

Although the National Advisory Commission on Criminal Justice Standards and Goals recommended in 1978 that plea bargaining be ***abolished***, the United States Supreme Court, instead, has moved toward granting ever-greater public legitimacy to the procedure. As discussed later in more detail, in the case of *North Carolina v. Alford* (1970),[6] the United States Supreme Court ruled that it was permissible for a trial court to accept a guilty plea, even though the defendant maintained his innocence, provided that there was some evidence of his guilt, and provided that there was no indication that he had been coerced. The defendant, while claiming to be innocent, had pleaded guilty to a lesser charge to avoid a risk of facing the death penalty. The plea was held valid because the accused had competent counsel whose advice was that the plea would be to the defendant's best interest. The following year in *Santobello v. New York* (1971),[7] the justices of the Supreme Court further endorsed the practice of plea bargaining by holding that the parties were required to keep the agreed-upon bargain.[8]

American jurisprudence is predicated upon three distinct sources of law: The Constitution, statutes and judicial opinions rendered by the courts. The Federal Rules of Criminal Procedure have the force of statutory law though they are drafted by judicial committees and promulgated by the United States Supreme Court. Rule 11(e) of the Federal Rules of Criminal Procedure (amended in 1974) brought plea negotiation into the open in the federal courts, establishing a procedure for presenting the terms. Rule 11(e)(1) states that:

> The attorney for the government and the attorney for the defendant or the defendant when acting pro se may engage in discussions with a view toward reaching an agreement that, upon the entering of a plea of guilty

> or nolo contendere to a charged offense or to a lesser or related offense, the attorney for the government will do any of the following:
>
> (A) move for dismissal of other charges; or
>
> (B) make a recommendation, or agree not to oppose the defendant's request, for a particular sentence, with the understanding that such recommendation or request shall not be binding upon the court; or
>
> (C) agree that a specific sentence is the appropriate disposition of the case.
>
> The court shall not participate in any such discussions.

Thus, Rule 11(e) provides parties with the authority to negotiate for plea agreements where the government will either dismiss charges, recommend sentencing, or agree to a specific sentence. Section (2) of Rule 11(e) deals with the requirements of notice of such an agreement:

> If a plea agreement has been reached by the parties, the court shall, on the record, require the disclosure of the agreement in open court or, on a showing of good cause, in camera, at the time the plea is offered. If the agreement is of the type specified in subdivision (e)(1)(A) or (C), the court may accept or reject the agreement, or may defer its decision as to the acceptance or rejection until there has been an opportunity to consider the presentence report. If the agreement is of the type specified in subdivision (e)(1)(B), the court shall advise the defendant that if the court does not accept the recommendation or request the defendant nevertheless has no right to withdraw his plea.

Section (3) of Rule 11 addresses what occurs when the court accepts a plea agreement:

> If the court accepts the plea agreement, the court shall inform the defendant that it will embody in the judgment and sentence the disposition provided for in the plea agreement.

And Section (4) explains what happens when the court rejects a plea agreement:

> If the court rejects the plea agreement, the court shall, on the record, inform the parties of this fact, advise the defendant personally in open court or, on a showing of good cause, in camera, that the court is not

> bound by the plea agreement, afford the defendant the opportunity to then withdraw his plea, and advise the defendant that if he persists in his guilty plea or plea of nolo contendere the disposition of the case may be less favorable to the defendant than that contemplated by the plea agreement.

Section (5) spells out the time to notify the court about a plea agreement:

> Except for good cause shown, notification to the court of the existence of a plea agreement shall be given at the arraignment or at such other time, prior to trial, as may be fixed by the court.

Finally, Section (6) of Rule 11 deals with the inadmissibility of pleas, plea discussions, and related statements in the event of a later trial. The section explains that:

> Except as otherwise provided in this paragraph, evidence of the following is not, in any civil or criminal proceeding, admissible against the defendant who made the plea or was a participant in the plea discussions.
>
> > (A) a plea of guilty which was later withdrawn;
> > (B) a plea of nolo contendere;
> > (C) any statement made in the course of any proceedings under this rule regarding either of the foregoing pleas; or
> > (D) any statement made in the course of plea discussions with an attorney for the government which do not result in a plea of guilty or which result in a plea of guilty later withdrawn.
> > However, such a statement is admissible (i) in any proceeding wherein another statement made in the course of the same plea or plea discussions has been introduced and the statement ought in fairness be considered contemporaneously with it, or (ii) in a criminal proceeding for perjury or false statement if the statement was made by the defendant under oath, on the record, and in the presence of counsel.[9]

Thus, the adoption of Rule 11 legitimized the case law approach to plea bargaining and codified the pre-existing rules into an established set of guidelines.

In 1968, prior to the adoption of Rule 11, the American Bar Association approved a set of standards relating to guilty pleas. The ABA's Standards Relating to Guilty Pleas concerned itself with such matters as the prosecutor engaging the defense attorney, judicial nonparticipation, judicial advisement of plea consequences, judicial concurrence in the disposition and affording similarly situated defendants equal bargaining opportunities. These safeguards, while not having the force of law, were meant to establish judicial scrutiny over the plea negotiations and to insure that the defendant made an informed and voluntary decision.[10]

Section 1.8 of the ABA standards entitled *Consideration of Plea in Final Disposition* explains that when the public's interest in the effective administration of criminal justice could be served, it is proper for the court to grant charge and sentence concessions to defendants who enter a plea of guilty or nolo contendere. The following considerations were to be taken into account in such a case:

> (i) whether the defendant by his plea has aided in ensuring the prompt and certain application of correctional measures to him;
>
> (ii) whether the defendant has acknowledged his guilt and shows a willingness to assume responsibility for his conduct;
>
> (iii) whether the concessions will make possible alternative correctional measures which are better adapted to achieving rehabilitative, protective, deterrent or other purposes of correctional treatment, or will prevent undue harm to the defendant from the form of conviction;
>
> (iv) whether the defendant has made public trial unnecessary when there are good reasons for not having the case dealt within a public trial;
>
> (v) whether the defendant has given or offered cooperation when such cooperation has resulted or may result in the successful prosecution of other offenders engaged in equally serious or more serious criminal conduct;

> (vi) whether the defendant by his plea has aided in avoiding delay (including delay due to crowded dockets) in the disposition of other cases and thereby has increased the probability of prompt and certain application of correctional measures to other offenders.

Section (b) of the ABA standards explains that:

> The court should not impose upon a defendant any sentence in excess of that which would be justified by any of the rehabilitative, protective, deterrent or other purposes of the criminal law because the defendant has chosen to require the prosecution to prove his guilt at trial rather than to enter a plea of guilty or nolo contendere.[11]

In addition, the passage of the Sentencing Reform Act of 1984[12] by the U.S. Congress marked the advent of mandatory minimum sentencing guidelines in federal courts in the United States. The mandatory minimum sentencing guidelines fundamentally changed the plea bargaining process in the federal courts in the United States by, in effect, shifting the sentencing role from the judge to the prosecutor in federal cases.[13] Before the enactment of the Sentencing Reform Act of 1984, federal judges had wide discretion in sentencing guilty defendants. After 1984, the sentencing discretion of federal judges was dramatically limited, due primarily to the requirement in the guidelines that judges sentence defendants convicted of certain serious federal crimes, such as drug trafficking, to a minimum, predetermined sentence.[14] As Jeffery Standen, a professor of law at Willamette University College of Law, states, "[t]oday is it the sentencing guidelines, rather then judge-determined sentences, that supply the parameters of plea bargaining."[15] The prosecutor's decision to charge defendants with certain crimes under the guidelines, enables the prosecutor to indirectly establish the sentence of the defendant.[16] Since the guidelines require minimum sentences for certain offenses, the decision to charge has also become a decision on sentencing by the prosecutor.[17]

After 1984, plea bargaining in federal courts has increasingly focused on "charge" bargaining, instead of sentence bargaining. The Sentencing Reform Act of 1984 did not alter or limit the wide charging discretion afforded prosecutors.[18] Critics charge that wide prosecutorial discretion undermines the Congressional intent of the Sentencing Reform Act of 1984 -- to reduce the wide disparity in sentencing in federal cases.[19] While sentences are predetermined for certain charges, the actual charges filed by the prosecutor are negotiable. Prosecutors realize that mandatory minimum sentences reduce the incentive to bargain on the part of defendants, which would inevitably lead to more trials and increased stress on an already overburdened criminal justice system.[20] As a result, prosecutors often charge defendants with less serious crimes which do not carry mandatory minimum sentences.[21]

JUDICIAL PRONOUNCEMENTS ON PLEA BARGAINING

The following discussion of significant cases demonstrates the increasing acceptance of plea bargaining by American Courts beginning at least as early as the 1960's. It also highlights the rationalization typically offered for the practice of plea bargaining by American courts. Plea bargaining practices apparently had not been addressed directly by the courts prior to the 1960's and, consequently, these cases represent a period of significant development in the rules that control the practice.

Prior to adoption of Rule 11(e) in 1969, the criteria for the acceptance of a guilty plea was discussed by the United States Supreme Court in *Marchibroda v. United States* (1969).[22] The standard established by the Court was that a plea would be void if it was "induced by promises or threats which deprived it of the character of a voluntary act."[23]

By 1969, however, perhaps due to pressures of urbanization and an increased crime rate,[24] the volume of criminal charges increased dramatically.[25] The Warren Court, then in its heyday of judicial activism, soon added elements to the *Marchibroda* formulation for acceptance of guilty pleas.[26] Specifically, in 1969 the Warren Court in *Boykin v. Alabama* (1969),[27] added two elements: (1) the entry of the plea must be knowledgeable (this would ensure that the defendant has full mental awareness of his or her decision) and (2) the trial court transcript must reflect these facts because the waiver of Sixth Amendment rights to trial by jury cannot be presumed from a "silent record."[28]

In some situations, practical considerations beyond the guilt or innocence of the accused were thought to taint the negotiation of a plea. In 1970, the United States Supreme Court in *Brady v. United States* (1970),[29] addressed such a circumstance and firmly endorsed the practice of plea bargaining. Brady had been indicted under Title 18 of the United States Code, section 1201(a), the federal kidnapping statute, which carried the possibility of death if recommended by the jury. Brady entered a plea of guilty rather than risk imposition of the death penalty pursuant to a jury trial. He was sentenced to 50 years in prison, but the sentence was later reduced to 30 years.

Thereafter, the Supreme Court in *United States v. Jackson* (1968),[30] held that the death penalty could not be imposed under the federal kidnapping statute. Several years later, Brady sought habeas corpus relief contending that the federal statute providing the imposition of the death penalty forced him into pleading guilty rather than risk exercising his constitutional right to trial. The court rejected Brady's claim that pleas entered "by the fear of the possible death penalty" are "invalid."[31]

Aside from reaffirming the constitutionality of plea bargaining in general, the court made two significant holdings with respect to defendants who plead guilty for the express purpose of avoiding the risk of capital punishment. First, the court held that the entry of a plea of guilty is not invalid if done for the purpose of avoiding the possibility of capital punishment provided the plea meets the voluntariness standard and is "entered by one fully aware of the direct consequences" of his plea.[32] Second, the Court held that Brady's plea was valid because it was based on competent advice of counsel, even though his attorney could not at the time have anticipated a change in the law providing for imposition of the death penalty. On this point the court stated:

> The voluntary plea of guilty intelligently made in the light of the then applicable law does not become vulnerable because later judicial decisions indicate that the plea rested on a faulty premise. A plea of guilty triggered by the expectation of the competently counseled defendant that the State will have a strong case against him is not subject to later attack because the defendant's lawyer correctly advised him with respect to the then existing law as to possible penalties but later pronouncements of the courts, as in this case, hold that the maximum penalty for the crime in question was less than was reasonably assumed at the time the plea was entered. . . . we find no requirement in the Constitution that a defendant must be permitted to disown his solemn admissions in open court that he committed the act with which he is charged simply because it later develops that the State would have had a weaker case than the defendant had thought or that the maximum penalty then assumed applicable has been held inapplicable in subsequent judicial decisions.[33]

A similar instance where an innocent defendant may decide to plead guilty is where the accused has a prior record but is innocent of the present charges. Prior to *Brady*, even though the Supreme Court had not set guidelines for the guilty plea process, an appeals court in California addressed such a situation in *Cortez v. United States* (1964), stating:[34]

> In a sense, it can be said that most guilty pleas are the result of a "bargain" with the prosecutor. But this standing alone does not vitiate such pleas. A guilty defendant must always weigh the possibility of his conviction on all counts, and the possibility of his getting the maximum sentence, against the possibility that he can plead guilty to fewer, or lesser, offenses, and perhaps receive a lighter sentence. The latter possibility exists if he pleads guilty to the whole charge against him. No competent lawyer, discussing a possible guilty plea with a client, could fail to canvass the possible alternatives with him. Nor would he fail to ascertain the willingness of the prosecutor to "go along." Moreover, if a codefendant is involved, and if the client is anxious to help that codefendant, a competent lawyer would be derelict in his duty if he did not assist in that regard. At the same time, the lawyer is bound to advise the client fully as to his rights, and to the alternatives available to him and of the fact that neither the lawyer nor the prosecutor nor anyone else can bargain for the court. There is nothing wrong, however, with a lawyer giving the client the benefit of his judgment as to what the court is likely to do, always making it clear that he is giving advice, not making a promise. The important thing is that there shall be no "deal" or "bargain" but that the plea shall be a genuine one, by a defendant who is guilty; one who understands his situation, his rights, and the consequences of the plea, and is neither deceived or coerced.[35]

A few years later, the United States Supreme Court, in *Brady*, recognized that the maintenance of the criminal justice system would be jeopardized if every defendant exercised their constitutional right to a trial. Similarly, in *Santobello v. New York* (1971),[36] the United States Supreme Court said:

> If every criminal charge were subjected to full scale trial, states and the Federal government would need to multiply by many times the number of judges and court facilities.[37]

In addressing the constitutionality of plea bargaining, the Supreme Court has explained that the Fifth and Sixth Amendment rights to silence and to a trial by jury equalize the contest between the state and the defendant and prevent the state from overwhelming the defendant.[38] These rights also provide a general check on the exercise of governmental power.

However, because plea bargaining may be used to pressure the defendant not to go to trial, it is inherently destructive of the values of the trial process. This concept is demonstrated in the Supreme Court cases of *Garrity v. New Jersey* (1967),[39] and *Spevak v. Klein* (1967).[40] The *Garrity* court held that incriminating evidence secured under the threat of discharge (for a government employee) is inadmissible. The *Spevak* court held that an attorney cannot be disbarred for failure to produce records and testify in a judicial inquiry if he had not been offered immunity from later criminal prosecution.[41] These cases say that the government cannot condition a benefit upon the furnishing of incriminating evidence and may not structure the defendant's choice such that he will forgo the Fifth Amendment privilege of silence under a narrow reading of this principal. Similarly, in *North Carolina v. Pearce* (1969),[42] the Supreme Court held that it violates due process to punish a defendant who appeals a conviction by meting out a harsher punishment upon reconviction. Again, broadly interpreted, this case supports the idea that differential sentencing based on noncorrectional factors may not be employed to deter the exercise of constitutional rights.[43] It has been suggested that if the abolition of plea bargaining requires such a drastic reallocation of resources as to disrupt basic social order, perhaps that is proof that the Fifth and Sixth Amendment guarantees are unworkable.

The Supreme Court in these cases has taken care to impose standards of conduct tending to minimize abuse in the negotiation of a guilty plea. The obvious potential for abuse, however, has not dampened the Court's enthusiasm for plea bargaining as a necessary expedient in the criminal justice system.

ENFORCEMENT OF THE BARGAIN: THE CONTRACT ANALOGY

In some respects, the basis of plea bargaining closely resembles the form of traditional contracts.[44] Many common law principles of contract law have been used by the Supreme Court and the lower courts to decide plea bargaining issues. Concepts of offer, acceptance, performance, breach, detrimental reliance, promissory estoppel and even the parole evidence rule have been used.[45] The manner in which the courts merge the contract analogy and the constitutional due process requirements are the source of dispute concerning plea negotiation breach.[46]

The following discussion traces the evolution of the contract analogy, in which a prosecutor promises the defendant something (i.e., recommendation for a light sentence), the judge does not follow the recommendation (i.e., imposes a heavier sentence), the defendant moves for a reduction of sentence pursuant to Rule 35(b), and the prosecutor opposes the motion, contrary to his original recommendation.[47] One question raised is whether this scenario of plea bargaining should be viewed from a contract standpoint, which would hold that the prosecutor is not obligated to repeat his recommendation (he only "contracted" to recommend a light sentence, not to leave a Rule 35(b) motion for sentence-reduction unopposed), or from a due process standpoint, which would hold that the defendant expected the prosecutor to keep his promise throughout the entire adjudication.[48]

A landmark case in the United States that addresses plea negotiation breach is *Santobello v. New York* (1971),[49] in which a broken plea bargain was brought before the Supreme Court. Following negotiations, the prosecutor agreed to permit the accused to plead guilty to a lesser included offense and to make no recommendation as to the sentence. When the case reached the sentencing stage, the prosecutor with whom the defendant had negotiated had been replaced, and the new prosecutor recommended the maximum sentence of one year. The defendant objected, but the judge, while assuring the defendant that the prosecutor's recommendation did not influence his sentencing, imposed the maximum sentence. The Supreme Court held that whether the recommendation had actually influenced the sentence was immaterial. The fact was that the defendant had been promised that no recommendation would be made, and that promise had not been kept.

Judicial interpretation of prosecutorial promises as they relate to sentence reduction motions was analyzed by the Fifth Circuit Court of Appeals in *United States v. Ewing* (1973).[50] There the prosecutor promised not to oppose probation, but when the defendant was sentenced to prison, the prosecutor opposed Ewing's sentence reduction motion. The court held that the prosecutor breached his promise -- opposing at sentence reduction proceedings is just like opposing it originally.[51]

In contrast, in *Bergman v. Lefkowitz* (1977),[52] the prosecutor promised the defendant a recommendation for concurrent sentences for state and federal offenses. The judge did not follow the recommendation and, at later sentence reduction proceedings, the prosecutor opposed. On appeal, the Second Circuit Court of Appeals held that the promise bound the prosecutor only for the original recommendation.[53]

In *Brooks v. U.S.* (1983),[54] the Seventh Circuit Court of Appeals rejected *Ewing* and followed a plain meaning approach to the interpretation of plea agreements.[55] The court held that "unless the agreement states otherwise, the prosecution is in no way constrained at a sentence-reduction proceeding by any promise to remain silent or make a positive recommendation at a sentencing hearing."[56] The court established a presumption that where the plea agreement does not specify otherwise, a promise by the government not to make a sentence recommendation does not bind the government after the original sentencing."[57]

In another important decision, *Mabry v. Johnson* (1984),[58] the United States Supreme Court weakened the contract analogy by holding that, where the defendant has not pleaded guilty or otherwise waived any constitutional rights in reliance on a plea bargain, the due process rights of the defendant are not violated.[59] Moreover, in *United States v. Robison* (1991),[60] the United States Sixth Circuit Court of Appeals ruled that a plea bargain was not breached by the prosecution when the defendant in North Carolina pleaded guilty for a reduced sentenced, but was then prosecuted on identical charges in Michigan.[61]

From the above cases, it is clear that most courts interpreting prosecutorial promises to recommend a specific sentence "have ruled that the prosecutor's promise does not extend to a Rule 35(b) [sentence reduction] motion."[62] Nonetheless, analogy to contracts may provide safeguards for both the defendant and the prosecution, while allowing the flexibility which is required in this area of the justice system.

Justification For And Criticisms Of Plea Bargaining

Plea bargaining may, in part, account for the numerous lists of crimes on the books, defined in minute detail and distinguished in several degrees. Rather than falling under a single broad definition, any given incident of criminal conduct may now easily be defined as illegal in any of several ways or degrees. One could argue that, as a result, we have an overdetermined system of law that requires the constant exercise of discretion and negotiation. Indeed, much of what is characterized as "plea bargaining" often involves the assessment and reassessment of facts to see how they fit under various definitions or categories of criminal offenses. Because many of these fine distinctions correlate to sentences of quite different length, there is an incentive for the accused to clarify these distinctions.

In theory, the courts determine the issue of guilt or innocence first and then consider the issues involved in sentencing. But with plea bargaining, the process of guilt determination is greatly affected by the substantive effects of conviction. Discretionary decisions early in the pre-trial process and negotiations leading to final case disposition all reflect a simultaneous sorting over both issues. Indeed, in the process of negotiation, participants frequently consider the question of punishment first. This is due partly to the fact that decisions about the charge are inextricably bound up with judgments about the appropriate sentence. But even more, this reversal of theoretical ordering of issues reflects the reality of the court in which facts are, to a large extent, "negotiated matters."[63]

In recent debates, plea bargaining has been criticized, on the one hand, for providing criminals with excessive leniency and, on the other hand, for coercing defendants to waive their constitutional rights to a trial.[64] Critics argue that plea bargaining is a symptom of an overcrowded system, operated to further the needs of the principal actors rather than the needs or interests of justice or the public.[65]

Plea bargaining is further criticized on the ground that parts of it are hidden from judicial scrutiny.[66] Because the bargain is generally made at an early stage of the proceedings, the judge may have little information about the crime or the defendant and is not always able to review prosecutorial judgment.[67] As a result, there is little judicial review of the methods used to arrive at the bargain, and no check on the amount of pressure applied to the defendant so that he or she plead guilty. Unconstitutional behavior may also be fostered. The police may engage in illegal searches, neglect the procedural rights of the defendant, and carry out station house punishment because they know that the case will never come to trial. As the President's Crime Commission has noted, "the result of bargain justice is that the judge, the public and sometimes even the defendant cannot know for certain who got what from whom in exchange for what."[68]

Proponents of plea bargaining are quick to point out that if the process is eliminated the judicial system will collapse. For example, Chief Justice Warren E. Burger of the United States Supreme Court has stated "that if the rate of criminal cases settled by guilty pleas were to decrease by 10% we would need twice as many judges and courtrooms."[69] In addition, recent attempts to ban plea bargaining (especially charge bargaining) in states like Alaska, have been unsuccessful.[70] Plea bargaining, even when outlawed, is still implicitly practiced by the major actors in the judicial system.[71]

Courts in the United States have advanced at least two rationales for adjusting sentences for those defendants who plead guilty to a reduced charge. First, is the belief that the defendant who pleads guilty is less culpable and thus less in need of rehabilitation than a defendant convicted after trial.[72] According to Manak, such a rationale is only valid where the plea is indicative of actual remorse for prior criminal acts; more likely, the accused is sorry to have been caught and wants to spend as little time as possible in prison or jail. The guilty plea therefore is primarily used for reasons of absolute self-interest and expediency rather than principle. The second rationale is that a defendant who pleads guilty is entitled to some discount in punishment because the plea aids in the efficient administration of justice. This rationale reflects practical administrative considerations having nothing to do with the defendant's prospects for reformation or other principles of punishment.[73]

VIEWS AND OBSERVATIONS ON THE ROLE OF THE PROSECUTOR

As the preceding discussion would suggest, the prosecutor is given tremendous discretionary authority in the American criminal justice system. As United States Courts of Appeals judge, Frank H. Easterbrook, states, the function of the broad discretionary power of prosecutors "is to obtain the optimum level of punishment at the least cost."[74] It has been said that prosecutorial discretion has probably saved the system from a premature and total "collapse."[75] According to Lundquist, prosecutorial discretion is thus upheld by the judiciary because, without it, the entire process would grind to an immediate halt.[76]

At first glance, it would seem natural that the prosecutor's office is used by some as a possible stepping stone to advancement in a future political career.[77] Because they often deal with dramatic, sensational materials, prosecutors can use the media to create a favorable climate of public opinion.[78] The prosecutor's discretionary power may be used so that the voters will be impressed with the prosecutor's abilities.[79] Charges may be dropped to avoid difficult cases, investigations initiated at politically opportune times and disclosures made of suspected wrongdoing by members of the opposition party.[80] Since they may be able to use their staff for campaigning work (even though this may be illegal), and hold offices where political contributions may be easily gathered, prosecutors may appear to be an irresistible force in local politics.[81] According to one assistant prosecutor:

> [The Prosecutor's] office represents a lot of political agencies of the county. For example, we represent the county commissioners. We represent all county officials, and we represent all judges, and by their

> very nature, these offices are political in that people have to run for their offices. In that sense, we are somewhat confronted with maybe certain political considerations . . .[82]

The power of prosecutors is enhanced by the circumstances under which they make decisions. Prosecutors in many states are elected on a partisan basis for a four-year term. There are few other public checks on their actions. In most states, the prosecutor is responsible either to no one other than the voters or only to the governor.[83] In addition, the decisions of the prosecutor are generally made outside the scrutiny of the public.[84] For example, a deputy prosecutor and a defense attorney may reach a verbal agreement over a cup of coffee or in the hall outside of the courtroom.[85]

Occasionally, the political nature of the position may constrain the prosecutor's discretion. Negotiations to encourage a plea of guilty to a lesser offense may be inhibited by the public notoriety that a case has received. Although the prosecutor would like to accept a plea to a lesser offense, the close public scrutiny awakened by the media may limit his freedom of action.[86]

The prosecutor has been called the most powerful single individual in the American judicial system.[87] In the United States, if the prosecutor does not act, the judge and the jury are helpless and the police officer's efforts are meaningless.[88]

Obviously, the prosecutor plays many roles, including crusader, administrator, counselor to other government officials and advocate. Each person occupying the position interprets the role differently, depending on the other parties to the relationship, the environment within which he or she operates, and his or her own personality.

When the prosecutor engages in plea bargaining, making concessions in return for the defendant's plea of guilty, he may assume one or more of the roles of administrator, advocate, judge or legislator. As an administrator, the prosecutor's primary goal is to dispose of cases in the fastest and most efficient manner in order to get his and the court's work done. Obviously, a trial is not the most efficient way of disposing of cases. In addition, the cases may be weak or raise questions of violations of the defendant's constitutional rights. Such problems evaporate when the prosecutor grants concessions to the accused and accepts a plea arrangement for a reduced charge or some other accommodation.

When the prosecutor functions as an advocate, he is attempting to either maintain or increase his conviction rate. While acting as advocate:

> the prosecutor must estimate the sentence that seems likely after a conviction at trial, discount this sentence by the possibility of an acquittal, and balance the "discounted trial sentence" against the sentence he can insure through a plea agreement.[89]

It would appear that the prosecutor would prepare to take this approach when he has a particularly strong case, but has insufficient time or motivation to try the case.

The prosecutor, while functioning as a judge, may attempt to do the "right thing" for the defendant by taking into account the defendant's social circumstances and relating them to the facts of the crime.[90] However, whether the prosecutor will grant concessions in order to do this depends upon the willingness of the defendant to plead guilty.[91] It would seem that when a prosecutor assumes the role of judge he may be violating his oath of office and his duty to his client, the state, as well as usurping the sentencing function of the judicial branch.[92]

As a legislator, the prosecutor, due to his broad discretion, may systematically refuse to prosecute specific crimes because, in his judgment, they either should not be criminal offenses in the first place or the prescribed punishments are too severe. When the prosecutor operates in such a fashion he is, in a sense, circumventing the will of the legislature.[93]

Many prosecuting attorneys have come to believe in the so-called "half loaf" philosophy of justice. According to this controversial view, one is better off plea bargaining and being sure of some punishment -- the "half loaf" -- rather than risking acquittal at trial.[94]

Since the government has access to police records at the early stages, which the defendant may not, the prosecutor is in a better position to know whether the evidence is likely to establish a conviction at trial.[95] Because of this gap in information, the prosecutor may be in a position to bluff the defendant into a guilty plea where the defendant would either have been acquitted or convicted of charges less serious than those to which he pleaded.[96] The informational gap can also cause inadequate representation for the defendant.[97] Public defenders, often saddled with overwhelming caseloads, as well as private attorneys working for low-income defendants, both have incentive to dispose of a case expeditiously.[98]

It has been said that the prosecutor can make the defense attorney's life pleasant or miserable by agreeing to or opposing continuances, by opening or closing files for discovery, by waiving or insisting on technical requirements, by recommending or denigrating the attorney to prospective clients, and by being generally agreeable or disagreeable.[99] Thus, defense attorneys at times are forced to abandon their adversarial stance in favor of accommodation.[100]

It is alleged that many prosecutors overcharge the defendant initially for the express purpose of charge bargaining.[101] At a later date, prosecutors intend to charge bargain down to the level which the defendant would probably be found guilty if the case went to trial.[102]

The reduction of a charge to a lesser included offense or the reduction of the number of charges, as a concession for a plea of guilty, is a major characteristic of the prosecuting process. The continual flow of guilty pleas and the corresponding avoidance of time, expense, and the uncertainty of trial are regarded by police, prosecutors, defense lawyers, and even judges as important factors in the efficient functioning of the criminal courts. The reduction of charges to lesser offenses as consideration for guilty pleas results in the disposition of a large number of cases without the usual demands on time and personnel made by the formalities of a trial. It represents an informal administrative device used to encourage guilty pleas and the consequent increased flow of case dispositions. The prosecutor will gauge his chances for success at trial on the charge originally laid against the speedy disposition of the case by a guilty plea on a reduced charge.[103]

Despite statutory provisions, there appears to be little state control over the freedom of local prosecuting attorneys to make these determinations. Debate in the United States has centered on the question whether it would be desirable to impose limitations on the exercise of prosecutorial discretion.[104] In analyzing the present practice of plea bargaining, it has been suggested that the prosecutor's two main reasons for plea bargaining are to save time and to improve his chances of conviction.

VIEWS AND OBSERVATIONS ON THE ROLE OF DEFENSE ATTORNEY

The defense attorney is a private practitioner who takes cases on his own initiative and is charged with representing the best interests of the accused. At times, however, the financial pressures of flat fees paid in advance and low hourly rates, along with heavy caseloads, puts pressure on defense attorneys to resolve cases quickly, through plea bargaining, without a trial.[105] In a judicial system where plea bargaining is a primary means of decision-making, it is not surprising that defense attorneys find it essential to have close personal ties with the police, the prosecutor and the other court officials. His or her professional survival, and the ability to serve his or her client's needs, may depend on the establishment and maintenance of good relations with these actors. At each point in the criminal process, from the first meeting with the accused until the final disposition of the case, the defense attorney is dependent on decisions made by others.

The criminal discovery process is an important ingredient in the plea bargaining process. In this process, the defense attorney and the prosecutor do not deal with each other from equal positions of strength. Rather, the prosecutor holds most of the cards. Prosecutors have access to resources, such as police investigators, government laboratories, professional legal staffs, an abundance of expert witnesses, and credibility among the general public.[106] As a result, the defense attorney, "because he lacks resources for conducting an independent investigation," must rely on one primary source of information -- the accused.[107]

Milton Heumann in his book, *Plea Bargaining* (1978), points out that some defense attorneys, if there is a chance the accused is innocent, use the tactic of maintaining their client is innocent throughout the first meeting with the prosecutor in an effort to get the prosecutor to dismiss the case. As a result, the main difference between negotiating a guilty plea and negotiating a dismissal is probably the defense attorney's perception of which of the two he or she should be working toward at that point in the negotiations. Depending upon these perceptions, the defense attorney might make a slight modification in what arguments and facts he or she presents to the prosecutor.

Another common tactic for negotiation by a defense attorney is to express a willingness and desire to go to trial to prove the defendant's innocence. This tactic is often only a bluff used to make the prosecutor offer a more lenient plea. Obviously, this tactic will result in some prosecutors periodically miscalculating the strength of the defendant's defense and, as a result, dismissing the case.

Defense counsel is not completely at the mercy of the state. At any phase in the proceedings, the defense has the ability to invoke the adversary model with its formal rules and public battles. The potential for an expensive, time-consuming and disputatious trial can be used by the effective counsel as a bargaining tool with the police, prosecutor and the judge.[108]

One of the most significant features of the 1973 report of the National Advisory Commission on Criminal Justice Standards and Goals was that, for the first time, an official body recognized that discretion played an important role in the administration of the criminal justice process. From the perspective of the Commission, discretion was the problem because it was exercised in an informal and invisible manner, often obscuring inefficiencies in the system and potentially treating citizens unfairly. To deal with this problem, the Commission concluded that discretion should be formalized and regularized through the creation of standards to guide decision-making. It was believed that, with published criteria, the visibility of the process would be raised and the faults of discretion would be corrected.[109] While the recommendations of this report were not immediately implemented, it made a positive contribution to later changes in the justice system.

VIEWS AND OBSERVATIONS ON THE ROLE OF THE PUBLIC DEFENDER

The public defender is a counterpart of the prosecutor. He or she is a government official but, instead of representing the people, the public defender represents the interests of indigent defendants.[110] Unlike most prosecutors, the public defender is typically not an elected official. Instead, the public defender usually is appointed by the judiciary or a county board.[111]

The reason for using an appointment system is quite simply the awkwardness of requiring an aspiring candidate for public defender to conduct a campaign -- "If I am elected more criminal defendants will go free and others will serve less time in prison."[112] While the candidate for the prosecutor's office can engage in a great deal of "law and order" rhetoric, promising to be tough on criminals, an aspiring public defender would be much more limited in what he or she could do to attract votes. Like many populous counties in the United States, the public defender's office of Cuyahoga County, Ohio, has a large caseload. Consequently, clients are represented by different attorneys at various stages of the judicial process. Clients do not have their own individual attorneys and cannot drop in for a review of their case in the office. Public defenders, who are often assigned to handle all matters before a specific judge for a length of time, realize that confrontations with their judge could make quite a difficult time. This may explain why one study found that private attorneys, as opposed to public defenders, received more favorable plea bargain offers for their clients. The implication is that "persons unable to afford the services of the private attorney must face more punitive or severe conditions as part of their plea bargaining agreement."[113]

The Cuyahoga County public defender's office was created in 1977. In 1997 it had a total of 80 employees, consisting of 32 attorneys, 4 social workers, 4 investigators, 5 law clerks, and various secretaries and intake clerks. The public defender's office consists of three divisions: a felony division, a juvenile division and an appellate division.

Public defenders are primarily responsible for representing those individuals who are unable to afford an attorney. The county public defenders handle approximately one-third of all the felony cases that are processed through the Cuyahoga County Common Pleas Court, which in the mid-1990's amounts to approximately 5,000 felony charges per year. They also handle post-conviction cases and parole and probation violation cases -- in an amount of approximately 500 to 600 per year. The office also handles around 300 appeals and around 1,500 juvenile cases. All told, they are *very* busy.[114]

According to the former chief county public defender:

> Our pressures, of course, are that we are limited with only 18 felony attorneys. . . . At times some of them are sick, at times some of them are on vacation, and therefore we only have anywhere from 13 to 15 attorneys any given day to handle 32 courtrooms. The prosecutor's office has approximately 50 to 60 attorneys handling those same courtrooms. They are assigned, to my understanding, three attorneys for every two courtrooms. We are assigned one attorney for every two courtrooms.[115]

Regarding plea bargaining, most public defenders do not think that the state is giving anything away in a plea bargaining situation. The county public defender explained that:

> Plea bargaining in the eyes of the public is that prosecution or the state is giving something away. In general they are giving nothing -- absolutely zero. Plea bargaining is trying to reduce the number of counts or charges against an individual and, in our eyes, the defense eyes, what the person should have been charged with originally, and the prosecution will dismiss certain counts or reduce certain charges on today's basis only and if they can't make their cases. So, they are not giving anything away. As a matter of fact, they are gaining something. Sometimes the evidence is so weak that they won't be able to make it, so they are giving a misdemeanant or they are knocking out a few of the major counts and reducing it to a lesser included offense. They are not giving away at all in today's system.[116]

The public defender system has been criticized because of the inadequate resources often provided to defendants, and because of the close relationships that sometimes exist between prosecutors and the public defenders.[117] It has also been suggested that, under the pressure of handling so many cases, public defenders not only become overtaxed, but soon feel that they are part of the state judiciary system, and thus may assume the prosecution's viewpoint.[118]

Justice for the defendant, therefore, may depend upon his or her own financial resources. Criminally accused individuals with money can hire high quality private defense attorneys, while indigent defendants must rely on public defenders paid for by the state. In 1902, Clarence Darrow told a group of inmates in Chicago that "[i]t will make little difference if you are guilty or innocent . . . [f]irst and last, it's a question of money."[119] This quote still rings true today. As David A. Harris states, "[o]nly those [defendants] with money [can] hire the lawyers, investigators and experts necessary to present a defense. For those without money, the criminal justice system [does] little but pronounce guilt."[120] Other legal scholars state that the chronic underfunding of public defenders has "nullified" the right to counsel for indigent defendants[121] recognized in the landmark United States Supreme Court case, *Gideon v. Wainwright* (1963).[122]

In contrast, the private practitioner is paid by his client and, hence, is in many respects more clearly on the client's side. The public defender, as stated earlier, is paid by the state, which would suggest he or she may be influenced.[123] Perhaps as a result, the operation of the system -- in the eyes of the defendants at least -- not only fails to teach moral lessons, but reinforces the idea that the system has no moral content.

Voucher systems in which the defendant is given something like a check and is then permitted to hire his own attorney, present a movement toward a more literal transaction between lawyer and client -- one that may be important in convincing the defendant that he has a lawyer who was on his side. Some kind of voucher system might also tend to alleviate the feeling of standing alone against a conspiracy that seems to permeate some public defender's system.[124]

Inequities in the system abound. Heumann observes that the more experienced defense attorneys are very likely to get their clients acquitted at trial due to their superior experience. He adds that, with a new prosecutor, the defense attorney often has a second goal of teaching the newcomer a lesson. In this regard, there is no such thing as a case that would definitely result in a conviction if it went to trial.[125]

According to Heumann, new lawyer socialization is the main reason why most attorneys develop a favorable attitude toward plea bargaining. A new attorney's expectations are not realistic. This causes temporary conflict within the system between veteran attorneys and newcomers. Gradually, the new lawyer is likely to discuss his problems with more experienced attorneys who have the same official role. The result is that newcomers slowly learn what specific cases are likely to result in conviction and how to plea bargain accordingly. Thus, attorneys are taught to prefer plea bargaining because it saves them work and, they come to believe, it often results in an outcome similar to what would have occurred if the case had gone to trial.

VIEWS AND OBSERVATIONS ON THE ROLE OF THE JUDGE

The bargaining system ultimately depends upon acceptance of the negotiated plea by the judge. It also requires that the judge fulfill the agreement by sentencing the accused according to the terms of the agreement. To put the agreement into effect, the judge and the defendant act out a little ritual in which statements are elicited to show that the guilty plea is made without reservations, and without the promise of leniency.[126]

American legal tradition maintains that a judge retain sentencing discretion so that he can tailor the punishment to the individual. This does not always work, however, when the legislature has preempted the judicial power by requiring that a mandatory nonsuspendable sentence be imposed. In this situation, the only way in which the defendant's counsel can help his guilty client secure more lenient treatment is to negotiate for a lesser charge.[127]

Ohio's version of Rule 11, entitled *Pleas, Rights Upon Plea*, sets the guidelines for court's acceptance of guilty pleas. Section (C)(2), pleas of guilty and no contest in felony cases, states:

> (2) In felony cases the court may refuse to accept a plea of guilty or a plea of no contest, and shall not accept such plea without first addressing the defendant personally and:
>
> (a) Determining that he is making the plea voluntarily, with understanding of the nature of the charge and of the maximum penalty involved, and, if applicable, that he is not eligible for probation.
>
> (b) Informing him of and determining that he understands the effect of his plea of guilty or no contest, and that the court upon acceptance of the plea may proceed with judgment and sentence.
>
> (c) Informing him and determining that he understands that by his plea he is waiving his rights to jury trial, to confront witnesses against him, to have compulsory process for obtaining witnesses in his favor, and to require the state to prove his guilt beyond a reasonable

> doubt at a trial at which he cannot be compelled to testify against himself.[128]

The role of the judge in plea bargaining differs from jurisdiction to jurisdiction. And, as previously mentioned, Federal district court judges are prohibited by the Federal Rules of Criminal Procedure, Rule 11(e)(1)(C), from participating in plea negotiations.[129] It is difficult to generalize, however, about the amount of participation the "average" judge has in plea bargaining. Although some argue that the judge does not usually play an important role in plea bargaining, nevertheless the judge is still a vital member for two reasons. First, the judge's formal role includes making sure that due process has been followed. A judge can refuse to accept a plea of guilty, thereby preventing the prosecution and defense attorney from successfully executing a plea agreement. There are several reasons why a judge may refuse to accept a plea of guilty.[130] In some cases, the defendant's plea may not be made voluntarily and knowingly or the factual basis for the charged crime may be missing. Similarly, the defendant may not realize the consequences of pleading guilty. In short, the judge is a key member at least for the reason that he has the power to stop the plea bargain.

A second reason why the judge can be vital is because experienced judges sometimes feel that the agreement is too lenient or too harsh. Consequently, the mere presence of the judge can operate as a check on the process since it becomes necessary for the defense attorney and the prosecutor to consider how the judge feels.[131]

Heumann points out that judges who lack experience on the bench gradually come to appreciate plea bargaining just as defense and prosecuting attorneys do.[132] Some judges refuse to participate at all while others become dominant figures during the negotiation.

Judges often admit that sentencing is the most difficult part of their jobs. There is no formal training on what sentences are appropriate for people convicted of various crimes and there are a variety of circumstances to take into consideration. Like a new attorney for the prosecution or the defense, the judge is often unsure of what a guilty party deserves as punishment. Often the judge finds himself in the position of having to decide whether or not to accept a plea agreement that contains a specific sentence. The fact that both of the adversaries concur in such an agreement is a powerful argument for accepting it. And, it seems reasonable if both adversaries agree to it. This makes the judge's job much easier. Not only does it eliminate the possibility of judicial error by eliminating a trial, but it often provides very explicit guidelines for sentencing. Finally, it also clears the judge's court calendar. The fact that plea bargaining is done informally eliminates even more work. It is not necessary to carefully record precisely what is stated.[133] Furthermore, a judge who refuses to bargain or refuses to accept bargains and thus "allows his calendar to lag will be cautioned by his presiding judge."[134]

The basic problem of judicial involvement in the procurement of a guilty plea is one of priority. The trial judge is expected to conduct himself so as to maintain "public confidence in the integrity and impartiality of the judiciary."[135] It is difficult to perceive how a judge can retain his impartiality when he actively or implicitly solicits guilty pleas. Thus, the consensus is that judges should neither implicitly or explicitly involve themselves in the plea bargaining process.[136] The American Bar Association has stated:

> A judge should not be a party to advance arrangements for the determination of sentence whether as a result of the guilty plea or finding of guilt based on proof.[137]

Alschuler points out that the main motive for judicial plea bargaining is the need to process large caseloads.[138] Judicial competition is another motive. As one Chicago prosecutor pointed out, "Around here, a judge's worth is measured by the number of cases that he can move, and it does not seem to matter how he moves them."[139] Furthermore, active judges are favored by most of the defense attorneys and many of the prosecutors. Basically, Alschuler feels that due to the pressures of caseload, superiors, etc., "the guilty-plea system usually tends to reduce itself to a common denominator -- the actively bargaining judge."[140]

A Cuyahoga County Common Pleas judge interviewed states that:

> If I had 25 cases a month, I couldn't try 25 cases a month. The pressure of the docket makes me and the prosecutor work on plea bargains. Plus you have the uncertainty of what a jury is going to do with a case. You know, every prosecutor's case is not as strong as the next one. So, on the weak cases, they're forced to plea bargain.[141]

He further explains that the statutory law contributes to the existing pressure in the system:

> If the defendant is in jail for 90 days before he is brought to trial, he can file a motion and his case has to be dismissed unless we have gotten a

waiver from him, and then a person not on bail has to be brought to trial within 270 days.[142]

According to one common pleas judge, another pressure that contributes to the use of more plea bargaining is the creation of the personal docket system. As explained by the judge:

> In 1969 Ohio adopted the so-called Modern Court Amendment which placed the rule-making power to govern the courts of Ohio directly in the Supreme Court's hands. The Modern Court Amendment placed the power to run the courts in the Supreme Court's hands and when they did that, Justice O'Neal of the Supreme Court set up commissions and established civil rules and criminal rules and established more importantly, the individual or personal docket. A criminal case at arraignment is assigned to a particular judge and that case stays with that particular judge until the case is finished. It used to be that, maybe one judge would handle certain motions, other judges would do other things and maybe couldn't tell who was going to end up handling the case.[143]

The personal docket system imposes individual accountability on the judges, which creates greater incentive to accept guilty pleas.

Some of the arguments against judicial involvement in plea bargaining include: the coercive nature of judicial plea bargaining; the possibility that a judge would not be able to conduct a fair trial in the event that negotiations had broken down; and the possibility that a judge would not be able to fairly gauge whether a defendant voluntarily waived his right to a trial. The most basic reason advanced against judicial participation or a commitment is that the judge's commanding position would influence or compel a defendant to waive his right to trial and to plead guilty when he was not guilty.[144]

Rationales in favor of judicial participation include the "practical necessity" of judicial participation, the "inevitability" of judicial participation, and the fact that most prosecutors and defense attorneys prefer judicial participation. A study completed by the Pennsylvania Criminal Procedural Rules Committee found that the advantages of allowing some limited judicial involvement in plea bargaining outweighs any potential for abuse.[145] According to the Committee, a judge can play an important role as a "neutral catalyst" between parties in a plea bargain to overcome an impasse in negotiations.[146] The Committee, however, states that a judge must not suggest to the defendant that a plea bargain should be negotiated or accepted.[147]

Once negotiations break down, especially if the defendant has expressed a willingness to tender a guilty plea, the presumption of innocence in the mind of the judge may be destroyed. In this situation, the most important question is how can a judge rule on objections to crucial items of evidence during the ensuing trial when, for some reason, the defendant was willing to plead guilty. The only saving grace may be that the defendant has requested a jury trial, but even this may be an insufficient safeguard. In the United States, jurors are judges of the facts, not of the law. Admissibility of evidence is a question of law. The judge determines whether an item of evidence is admissible while the jury merely evaluates it. Of course, the trial judge may argue that this is a situation analogous to that in which he must rule on the admissibility of a confession.

Judge Thomas Lambros, retired Chief Judge of the United States District Court for the Northern District of Ohio, has indicated several reasons in support of judicial participation in plea discussion. For one, it provides the defendant and defense counsel with additional facts and factors for consideration in the total evaluation of whether a plea of guilty should or should not be entered. As a consequence, the defendant does not plead in the dark.[148] Judge Lambros further suggests that the plea becomes more meaningful and informed in two respects. First, judicial participation in plea discussion inevitably causes the prosecutor to open his file and to freely discuss the strength of his case. Second, judicial participation is more meaningful and informed as a result of discussion as to the sentencing alternatives.

Some also believe that judicial involvement in plea discussions expedites litigation and in turn reduces the backlog of cases.[149] Judicial involvement in plea discussions also provides the judge a vehicle through which he can acquire additional information so as to supplement the report of the probation department.

One judge, explaining the plea bargaining process in Ohio, stated:

> One of the things about plea bargaining in Ohio, [is that] the legislature is set up so that maybe one act could result in three, four, or five crimes. So, if somebody is indicted for the five crimes, resulting from one or two acts, the fact that they are allowed to plead guilty to two counts and three counts were nolle, is a good plea . . . Because if they were found guilty of all five counts and were sentenced to jail, they would do more time because they've got five counts than they would if they've got two

counts. And you have to understand that before you can understand plea bargaining.[150]

As seen in the next chapter, the operation of the criminal justice system in Canada differs in several key respects from that of the United States. These differences, together with differences in the governing rules of conduct, result in a vastly different plea negotiation practice.

NOTES

1. Hyman Friedman, Cuyahoga County Chief Public Defender at the time of the interview, interview by author, tape recording, Cleveland, Ohio, 1987.

2. Kamisar, LaFave, and Israel, *Modern Criminal Procedure*.

3. Alan Rossman, Cuyahoga County Public Defender, interview by author, tape recording, Cleveland, Ohio, 1987.

4. Kenneth E. White, "*Mabry v. Johnson*: The Supreme Court Sees the Forest Through the Trees, Reverses Plea Bargain Decision," *The American Journal of Trial Advocacy* 8 (1984-85): 266-292.

5. Samuel Walker, "Exploring the Roots of Our Criminal Justice Systems," *Michigan Law Review* 81 (1982-83): 946-952.

6. *North Carolina v. Alford*, 400 U.S. 25 (1970).

7. *Santobello v. New York*, 404 U.S. 257 (1971).

8. Walter E. Hoffman, "Plea Bargaining and the Role of the Judge," Federal Rules Decisions 53 (1971) 499.

The reasons for the development of plea bargaining practice are perhaps best summarized in the remarks of President Richard M. Nixon to the National Conference of the Judiciary on March 11, 1971. In speaking on the unconscionable delays in criminal cases he said:

> overcrowded penal institutions, unremitted pressure on judges and prosecutors to process cases by plea bargaining without the safeguards recently set forth by the American Bar Association, the clogging of the court calendars of inappropriate and relatively unimportant matters -- all of this sends everyone in the system of justice home at night feeling as if he had been trying to brush back a flood with a broom.

9. Federal Criminal Code and Rules, "Rule 11(e)(1)(c)" (St. Paul, Minn.: West Publishing Company, 1994), 40. *See also* Branford C. Mank, "Broken Promises and Involuntary Confessions: May a State Introduce Incriminating Statements Made by a Defendant as a Result of Promises in a Plea Bargain Agreement if the Defendant Breaches that Agreement?," *Cleveland State Law Review* 36 (1988): 423-440.

10. "The Unconstitutionality of Plea Bargaining," *Harvard Law Review* 83 (1969-70): 1387.

11. American Bar Association, *Project on Minimum Standards for Criminal Justice, Standards Relating to Guilty, Pleas of Guilty* (1968): 8-9, 36-37, 37-52.

12. Sentencing Reform Act of 1984 (Title II of the Comprehensive Crime Control Act of 1984), 28 U.S.C. section 991 (1988). The Sentencing Reform Act was created by the United States Sentencing Commission whose mandate is to write and monitor the mandatory sentencing guidelines. *See* Julie Gyurci, "Prosecutorial Discretion to Bring a Substantial Assistance Motion Pursuant to a Plea Agreement: Enforcing a Good Faith Standard," *Minnesota Law Review* 78 (1994): 1253-1283.

13. Thomas E. Zeno, "A Prosecutor's View of the Sentencing Guidelines," *Federal Probation* (December 1991): 32.

14. Ibid., 31-32.

15. Jeffrey Standen, "Plea Bargaining in the Shadow of the Guidelines," *California Law Review* 81 (1993): 1475.

16. Ibid.

17. Zeno, "Prosecutor's View," 31-32.

18. Standen, "Plea Bargaining," 1474-1475.

19. Harvey Berkman, "Court To Take On Sentencing Rules," *The National Law Journal*, 15 January 1996, A21.

20. Rudolph J. Gerber, "Symposium: Violence, Crime and Punishment," *Saint Louis University Public Law Review* 12 (1993): 225-227.

21. Ibid.

22. *Marchibroda v. United States*, 386 U.S. 487 (1969).

23. Ibid., 493.

24. Addressed in more detail later in this study.

25. Theodore S. Greene, John D. Wood, and Allan Arcuri, "Plea Bargaining: Fairness and Inadequacy of Representation," *Columbia Human Rights Law Review* 7 (Fall/Winter 1975-76): 495-527.

26. Ibid.

27. *Boykin v. Alabama*, 395 U.S. 238 (1969).

28. Ibid., 242.

29. *Brady v. United States*, 397 U.S. 742 (1970).

30. *United States v. Jackson*, 390 U.S. 570 (1968).

31. *Brady v. United States*, 397 U.S. 742, 755 (1970).

32. Ibid., 755.

33. Ibid., 757.

34. *Cortez v. United States*, 337 F.2d 699 (1964). Another instance of a possibly innocent person avoiding the risk of the death penalty can be seen in *North Carolina v. Alford*, 400 U.S. 25 (1970), where the defendant, while claiming to be innocent, pleaded guilty to a lesser charge to avoid the death penalty. The plea was held valid because the accused had competent counsel whose advice was that the plea would be in the defendant's best interest.

35. Ibid.

36. *Santobello v. New York*, 404 U.S. 257 (1971).

37. Ibid., 260.

38. "Unconstitutionality of Plea Bargaining," 1395-1396.

39. *Garrity v. New Jersey*, 385 U.S. 493 (1967).

40. *Spevak v. Klein*, 385 U.S. 511 (1967).
41. "Unconstitutionality of Plea Bargaining," 1399.
42. *North Carolina v. Pearce*, 395 U.S. 711 (1969).
43. "Unconstitutionality of Plea Bargaining," 1402
44. White, "*Mabry v. Johnson*," 267. *See also* Graham Hughes, "Agreements for Cooperation in Criminal Cases," *Vanderbilt Law Review* 45 (1991): 1-69.
45. White, "*Mabry v. Johnson*," 267.
46. David E. Rovella, "Fake Plea Bargain in Death Case Raises Concerns," *The National Law Journal*, 9 October 1995, A13.
47. Daniel F. Kaplan, "Where Promises End: Prosecutorial Adherence to Sentence Recommendation Commitments in Plea Bargains," *The University of Chicago Law Review* 52 (1985): 751.
48. Ibid.
49. *Santobello v. New York*, 404 U.S. 257 (1971).
50. *U.S. v. Ewing*, 480 F.2d 1141 (5th Cir. 1973).
51. Kaplan, "Where Promises End," 759.
52. *Bergman v. Lefkowitz*, 569 F.2d 705 (2nd Cir. 1977).
53. Kaplan, "Where Promises End," 760.
54. *Brooks v. U.S.*, 708 F.2d 1280 (7th Cir. 1983).
55. Kaplan, "Where Promises End," 761.
56. Ibid., 762.
57. Ibid., 763.
58. *Mabry v. Johnson*, 467 U.S. 505 (1984).
59. Ibid., 506. *See* William M. Ejzak, "Plea Bargains and Nonprosecution Agreements: What Interests Should Be Protected When Prosecutors Renege?," *University of Illinois Law Review* 1991 (1991): 107-136.
60. *United States v. Robison*, 924 F.2d 612 (6th Cir. 1991).
61. Ibid., 613-614. *See* James P. Arrigo, "*United States v. Robison* and the Enforcement of Plea Bargains Across Federal Jurisdictional Lines: To Bind or Not to Bind?," *DePaul Law Review* 43 (1994): 909-962.
62. Kaplan, "Where Promises End," 772.
63. Lynn M. Mather, *Plea Bargaining or Trial: The Process of Criminal Case Disposition* (Lexington, Mass.: D.C. Heath Company, 1979), 141; Lynn M. Mather, "Some Determinants of the Methods of Case Disposition," *Law and Society Review* 8 (1974): 188.
64. Robert E. Scott and William J. Stuntz, "Plea Bargaining as Contract," *Yale Law Journal* 101 (1992): 1918-1919.
65. Bureau of Justice Statistics, *Felony Case Processing Time* (Washington, D.C.: U.S. Government Printing Office, 1986).
66. David A. Starkweather, "The Retributive Theory of 'Just Deserts' and Victim Participation in Plea Bargaining," *Indiana Law Journal* 67 (1992): 858-859.
67. Ibid., 867-868.
68. *See* Packer, *Criminal Sanction*.

69. Warren E. Burger, "The State of the Judiciary," *American Bar Association Journal* 56 (October 1970): 929-934.
70. Teresa W. Carns and John Kruse, "A Re-evaluation of Alaska's Plea Bargaining Ban," *Alaska Law Review* 8 (1991): 65.
71. Ibid., 66.
72. *See* Lynch, "Impropriety of Plea Agreements," 115-116.
73. James Manak, "Plea Bargaining: The Prosecutor's Perspective" (National District Attorney's Association, 1973), 4-5.
74. Frank H. Easterbrook, "Plea Bargaining as Compromise," *Yale Law Journal* 101 (1992): 1980.
75. John A. Lundquist, "Prosecutorial Discretion: Reevaluation of the Prosecutors Unbridled Discretion and its Potential for Abuse," *DePaul Law Review* 21 (Winter 1971): 515.
76. Ibid.
77. Lawrence Fleischer, "Thomas E. Dewey and Earl Warren: The Rise of the Twentieth Century Urban Prosecutor," *California Western Law Review* 28 (1991): 4.
78. Stacia L. Haynie and Ernest A. Dover, "Prosecutorial Discretion and Press Coverage: The Decision to Try the Case," *American Politics Quarterly* 22 (1994): 372.
79. William T. Pizzi, "Understanding Prosecutorial Discretion in the United States: The Limits of Comparative Criminal Procedure as an Instrument of Reform," *Ohio State Law Journal* 54 (1993): 1345.
80. Ibid.
81. Fleischer, "Urban Prosecutor," 1-2.
82. George Sadd, Assistant County Prosecutor and Chief of the Appeals Division for Cuyahoga County at the time of the interview, interview by author, tape recording, Cleveland, Ohio, 1987.
83. Pizzi, "Understanding Prosecutorial Discretion," 1337.
84. Ibid.
85. Herbert Packer, "Two Models of the Criminal Process," *University of Pennsylvania Law Review* 113 (Nov. 1964): 1-68. *See also* Packer, *Criminal Sanction*.
86. Haynie and Dover, "Prosecutorial Discretion and Press Coverage," 379.
87. Haynie and Dover, "Prosecutorial Discretion and Press Coverage," 370.
88. Kenneth J. Melilli, "Prosecutorial Discretion in an Adversary System," *Brigham Young University Law Review* 1992 (1992): 671-672.
89. Albert W. Alschuler, "The Prosecutor's Role in Plea Bargaining," *University of Chicago Law Review* 36 (Fall 1968): 52.
90. J. Langley Miller and John J. Sloan, III, "A Study of Criminal Justice Discretion," *Journal of Criminal Justice* 22 (1994): 108.
91. Alschuler, "Prosecutor's Role in Plea Bargaining," 53.
92. Miller and Sloan, "Criminal Justice Discretion," 120.
93. Pizzi, "Understanding Prosecutorial Discretion," 1337.

94. Herbert S. Miller, William McDonald, and James Kramer, *Plea Bargaining in the United States* (Washington, D.C.: U.S. Government Printing Office, 1978).

95. Eleanor J. Ostrow, "The Case for Preplea Disclosure," *The Yale Law Journal* 90 (1981): 1583.

96. Donald J. Rose, "Prosecutorial Misconduct," *Georgetown Journal of Legal Ethics* 6 (1993): 1086.

97. Ostrow, "Preplea Disclosure," 1584.

98. Ibid., 1587.

99. Alan M. Dershowitz, *The Best Defense* (New York: Vantage Books, 1983), 355.

100. Ibid.

101. *See* Miller, MacDonald, and Kramer, *Plea Bargaining*.

102. Eric Stringfellow and Joseph D. Rice, "An Indictment of the System: Cuyahoga Track Record Hints of Overcharging," *Cleveland Plain Dealer*, 30 April 1991, 1-C. For example, in Cleveland, prosecutors who prepare indictments alleging the passing of bad checks generally charge the accused with not only one, but three offenses for each bad check -- forgery, uttering and obtaining property by false pretense.

103. *See* Grosman, *Exercise of Discretion*.

104. Ibid., 31.

105. Stephen J. Schulhofer, "A Wake-up Call from the Plea-Bargaining Trenches," *Law and Social Inquiry* 19 (1994): 138.

106. Kenneth B. Nunn, "The Trial as Text: Allegory, Myth and Symbol in the Adversarial Criminal Process -- A Critique of the Role of the Public Defender and a Proposal for Reform," *American Criminal Law Review* 32 (1995): 745.

107. Steven L. Friedman, "Pre-Plea Discovery: Guilty Plea and the Likelihood of Conviction at Trial," *University of Pennsylvania Law Review* 119 (January 1971): 527-535.

108. *See* Miller, MacDonald, and Kramer, *Plea Bargaining*, 6.

109. "A Thoughtful Examination of Some of the Major Criminal Justice Issues, with Recommendations for Change," in *Struggle for Justice. A Report on Crime and Punishment in America*, (New York: Hill & Wang, 1971).

110. Nunn, "Trial as Text," 788.

111. David A. Sadoff, "The Public Defender as Private Offender: A Retreat from Evolving Malpractice Liability Standards for Public Defenders," *American Criminal Law Review* 32 (1995): 887.

112. Dean J. Champion, "Private Counsels and Public Defenders: A Look at Weak Cases Prior to Records and Leniency of Plea Bargaining," *Journal of Criminal Justice* 17 (1989): 253-263.

113. Ibid.

114. Cuyahoga County Public Defender office supervisor, interview by author, Cleveland, Ohio, 1997.

115. Friedman, interview.

116. Ibid.

117. Emily Rubin, "Ineffective Assistance of Counsel and Guilty Pleas: Toward a Paradigm of Informed Consent," *Virginia Law Review* 80 (1994): 1706.

118. Sadoff, "Public Defender as Private Offender," 888.

119. Harris, "The Constitution and Truth Seeking," 469.

120. Ibid. *See also* Paul Calvin Drecksel, "The Crisis in Indigent Defense," *Arkansas Law Review* 44 (1991): 363-401.

121. Andrew Blum, "Defense of Indigents: Crisis Spurs Lawsuits," *The National Law Journal*, 15 May 1995, A1.

122. *Gideon v. Wainwright*, 372 U.S. 335 (1963).

123. David J. Richards, "The Public Defender Defendant: A Model Statutory Approach to Public Defender Malpractice Liability," *Valparaiso University Law Review* 29 (1994): 521-522.

124. Jonathan D. Casper, "Did You Have a Lawyer When You Went to Court? No, I had a Public Defender," *Yale Review of Law and Social Action* 1 (Spring 1971): 4-9.

125. Milton Heumann, *Plea Bargaining: The Experience of Prosecutors, Judges and Defense Attorneys* (Chicago: University of Chicago Press, 1978).

126. George F. Cole, *Politics and the Administration of Justice* (Beverly Hills, Calif.: Sage Publications, 1973), 203.

127. Ibid., 206.

128. Ohio Rules of Criminal Procedure, "Rule 11, Pleas, Rights Upon Plea," *Rules Governing the Courts of Ohio* (Cincinnati: Anderson Publishing Company, 1994/95), 90.

129. Federal Criminal Code and Rules, "Rule 11(e)(1)(c)" (St. Paul, Minn.: West Publishing Company, 1994), 40.

130. *See* Miller, MacDonald, and Kramer, *Plea Bargaining.*

131. *See* Arthur Rosett and Donald Cressey, *Justice by Consent: Plea Bargains in the American Courthouse* (Philadelphia: Lippincott & Company, 1976).

132. *See* Heumann, *Prosecutors, Judges and Defense Attorneys.*

133. Karen Rebrovich, "Factors Effecting the Plea Bargaining Process in Erie County: Some Tentative Findings," *Buffalo Law Review* (Fall 1977): 693-711.

134. Jerome H. Skolnick, "Social Control in an Adversary System," *Journal of Complex Resolution* 11 (March 1967): 52-70.

135. American Bar Association, *American Bar Association Code of Professional Responsibility and Code of Judicial Conduct* (Chicago: American Bar Association, 1974).

136. Albert W. Alschuler, "The Trial Judges Role in Plea Bargaining," *Columbia Law Review* 76 (November 1977): 1059-1154.

137. Informal Opinions of the Professional Ethics Committee, *American Bar Association Journal* 51 (May 1965): 444.

138. Alschuler, "Trial Judges Role," 1099.

139. Ibid., 1100.

140. Ibid., 1102.

141. Frank Gorman, Cuyahoga County Common Pleas Court Judge, interview by author, tape recording, Cleveland, Ohio, April 8, 1987.

142. Ibid.

143. Ibid.

144. *Elksnis v. Gilligan*, 256 F.Supp. 244 (SDNY 1966).

145. "Comment to the Amended Rule Changes Concerning Judicial Involvement in Plea Agreements," *Pennsylvania Law Weekly*, 15 January 1996, 11.

146. Ibid.

147. Ibid.

148. *Brown v. Peyton*, 435 F.2d 1352 (4th Cir. 1970).

149. *Commonwealth v. Evans*, 432 Pa. 52, 252 A.2d 689 (1969) (Dissenting Opinion).

150. Frank Gorman, interview.

CHAPTER 3
THE WELL-ESTABLISHED BUT LESS ACCEPTED PRACTICE IN CANADA

Little study has been made of plea negotiation in Canada. Far more research on plea negotiation has been conducted in the United States. Any attempt to generalize these research findings to Canada would be a mistake, however, not only because of the difference in their structure, but also because the basis of Canada's legal system differs from the United States.

One fundamental difference between the two countries can be seen in a reference made by Packer to the nature of the United States system:

> [Canada's] is not a system of legislative supremacy. The distinctively American institution of judicial review exercises a limiting and ultimately a shaping influence on the criminal process.[1]

In the United States, some of the limits which are placed on the nature of official power and on the modes of its exercise are derived from judicial review, supra-legislative law which is based upon the United States Constitution. Canada does not have in its law the equivalent of such landmark decisions of the U.S. Supreme Court -- *Escobedo v. Illinois*, *Mapp v. Ohio*, *Gideon v. Wainwright*, *Miranda v. Arizona*, etc. This should not be construed as meaning that Canada is not concerned about the problems these decisions address. Rather, it means that the foundation of the legal system itself is quite different, resulting in fundamentally different rights of an accused.

General Background: The Roles Of The Actors

The practice of "plea negotiations," as Canadians refer to it, cannot be considered without a firm understanding of the objectives of the criminal justice system and the roles of its leading participants and the court. In Canada, criminal law and procedure are federal matters, enforced by provincial officials in provincial courts, presided over by federally appointed judges. According to the Canadian Constitution, the Queen, by and with the advice of the Senate and House of Commons, may make laws with respect to all matters not coming within the scope of the provincial legislatures. The provinces may enact legislation dealing with the imposition of punishment, by fine, penalty, or imprisonment, for enforcing any law of the province within the scope of the provincial jurisdiction. Crown attorneys have the responsibility for the administration of justice in the provinces.

The Attorney General of Canada is entrusted with the same powers and charged with the same duties that belong to the office of the Attorney General of England. The Attorney General of Canada has responsibility for the regulation and conduct of all litigation for or against the Crown or any public department.[2]

The practice of plea negotiations is not as well entrenched in Canada as it is in the United States. A Canadian commentator states that:

> Bargaining has never been fully recognized as a legitimate practice in Canada, at least not to the same extent as in some American jurisdictions. There is by no means a uniform set of rules governing this process, and the way it functions depends primarily on the kinds of relationships that have grown up between magistrates, Crown attorneys and defense counsel in particular parts of the province.[3]

THE ROLE OF THE CROWN ATTORNEY

In contrast to the United States, where some district attorneys and prosecutors take an active role in the investigative process similar to that of a policeman or detective, Canadian Crown attorneys stay away from this practice. Perhaps this is due to the fact that in Canada the police usually set the prosecution process in motion. Crown attorneys are clearly expected to control police prosecution decision-making, and they have been provided with power to do so, but a Crown attorney generally does not become aware of a prosecution until after the police have completed their job.

There are two types of criminal cases in Canada, police cases and government department created cases. While the prosecutor reviews each government case before a charge is laid, the police are free in police cases to exercise their discretion in deciding to charge someone, in choosing the charge, and in other initial basic decisions. The Crown's office does not intervene in their cases at that initial stage.

When the police decide to prosecute, they send a referral to the Crown attorney's office prior to the charge being laid. This is when the Crown's office first becomes involved. The charge is laid and the accused comes to court (arraignment). The police are supposed to provide the Crown with a brief of all the evidence within sixty days of the arrest. These briefs are reviewed by the Crown office. If, in the process of this review, they determine that the charge should be reduced, they have the responsibility of contacting the police and instructing them to lay a new charge to replace the first charge. So, while there is intervention at a fairly early stage, it is not as early as in the government cases.[4]

THE ROLE OF THE DEFENSE ATTORNEY AND THE LEGAL AID ATTORNEY

Canada operates a legal aid system to assist indigent defendants. This is different from the public defender system in the United States. In Canada, if a defendant qualifies, he is entitled to a legal aid certificate. A legal aid certificate entitles one to hire a lawyer of his own choice, provided that the attorney he chooses agrees to take the case. The attorney, should he accept the case, will be paid by the legal aid plan. This system is not only supported by the people and the government, but the legal profession also contributes financially to the legal aid system.

If the defendant decides to plead guilty, the defense attorney or the legal aid attorney, which is basically the same, will make an appointment to see the Crown attorney. Usually at this meeting both parties will discuss and determine what sentence would be appropriate for the offense committed. Basically, what the accused wants to know in this meeting is what the judge is going to do, not so much what the Crown or the defense is going to say.

The next step for the defense attorney is to make an appointment with the "pretrial" judge and crown attorney. At this informal meeting, the defense counsel will notify the pretrial judge whether his client wants a trial and will explain to the judge what the case is all about. He will also make a recommendation to the pretrial judge as to what type of sentence he thinks the defendant should get if he is pleading guilty.[5]

THE ROLE OF THE JUDGE

Unlike many cases in the United States, in Canada the pretrial judge is not the same person as the trial judge. The purpose of a pretrial conference with a different judge is to enable the two sides (defense attorney and the Crown) to discuss the case with a judge without fear of compromising the case in any way because the main role of the pretrial judge is to assist them in the discussion. The purpose of this conference is to resolve issues. This may lead to a guilty plea, but that is not the primary purpose of the conference. In this conference, if the Crown and the defense come to some agreement on what they think is appropriate as a plea, the judge then will often indicate whether, as a judge, he would find that acceptable. If he thinks the proposition is acceptable, both parties may make an arrangement to enter the plea before the same judge if all parties are agreeable. If at any point in the pretrial conference the judge does not agree with the Crown and the defense, he may intervene and tell both sides that they will not be able to convince any judge to rule as they desire. While the pretrial judge will try to get both sides together, neither the pretrial judge nor the judge who will ultimately hear the case is obligated to accept the joint submission of the defense and Crown.[6]

CANADIAN CHARTER OF RIGHTS AND FREEDOMS

On April 17, 1982, the Canadian Charter of Rights and Freedoms (hereinafter referred to as "the Charter") was added to the Canadian Constitution, resulting in increased rights for the criminally accused.[7] For instance, section 8 of the Charter states. Section 8 of the Charter states: "[e]veryone has the right to be secure against unreasonable search or seizure." In addition, the Charter contains an exclusionary rule in section 24(2) to prohibit the admission into court of evidence that "would bring the administration of justice into disrepute."

Another area expanded by the adoption of the Charter is the right of criminally accused individuals to obtain legal representation after being detained by law enforcement personnel. Section 10(b) of the Charter states: "[e]veryone has the right on arrest or detention . . . to retain and instruct counsel without delay and to be informed of that right." Violation of this Charter provision by police officers may result in the exclusion of probative evidence from court through the application of the exclusionary rule in section 24(2).[8]

The Canadian Charter of 1982 marks the most recent substantive addition to the Canadian Constitution. The Canadian Constitution came into existence as a result of the enactment of the Constitution Act, 1867.[9] The Constitution Act, 1867, united the separate colonies of British North America into a federal system consisting of one federal government and various provincial governments.[10] In addition, the Constitution Act, 1867, created a unitary court system based on the principles of parliamentary sovereignty.[11] In other words, the Canadian Parliament created by the Act was supreme to other centers of power and authority, including the courts. Thus, a law passed by the Parliament impacting plea bargaining could not be challenged in the court system because the courts lacked the power of judicial review.

The Constitution Act, 1867, however, contained no "bill of rights" guaranteeing the individual rights of Canadians.[12] As a response to this situation, the Diefenbaker government in 1960 enacted the Canadian "Bill of Rights".[13] The Canadian "Bill of Rights" was enacted as an ordinary statute of Parliament that recognized "the political civil liberties of speech, religion, assembly, association and the press along with due process and equality before the law."[14] The guarantees set forth by the Canadian "Bill of Rights" were not entrenched into the Canadian Constitution, and were thus applicable only to federal laws.[15] As a consequence of existing as an act of Parliament, the "Bill of Rights" could be overturned at any time by that legislative body.[16]

The idea of formally entrenching the rights of individuals into the Canadian Constitution became an important issue for Prime Minister Pierre Trudeau in 1982 because of the divisive separation referendum held in Quebec in 1980.[17] Trudeau stated that constitutionally entrenched individual liberties "would enhance national unity by emphasizing what Canadians hold in common -- citizenship -- now to be defined by a common set of rights against both levels of government."[18] Trudeau's dream of constitutionally entrenched individual rights became a reality with the enactment of the Charter in 1982. The Charter comprised the first section of the Constitution Act, 1982, which formally ingrained individual rights into the Canadian Constitution.[19] The Constitution Act, 1982, patriated the Canadian Constitution and ended formal British influence in the governance of Canada. The Canadian judicial system, however, continues to maintain adherence to the English common law system.[20]

After the enactment of the Charter in 1982, the Canadian judicial system increasingly adopted features of Packer's due process model of justice.[21] For instance, courts under section 24(2) of the Charter had the discretion of exclude probative evidence from trial if the judge believed that the manner in which the evidence was gathered, according to section 24(2), "would bring the administration of justice into disrepute." Before 1982, all evidence, including illegally obtained evidence, was admissible in court under the common law.[22] The common law permitted the introduction of all evidence as long as it directly pertained to the case being tried. Section 24(2) of the Charter abrogated the common law in the area of the admission of illegally obtained evidence, thus creating a potential obstacle for Canadian law enforcement personnel to overcome.

The Charter is reshaping the Canadian criminal justice system. The Charter provisions, such as section 24(2), play an important role in deterring illegal conduct by the police and help to prevent the prosecution from benefitting from such unlawful conduct.[23] In addition, the Charter provisions force law enforcement personnel to perform thorough and careful investigative work that strengthens the prosecution's case and makes the advantages of a plea bargain look more attractive to a defendant than going through an uncertain trial.[24] Under section 11(d)[25] of the Charter, if a defendant feels that a plea agreement is unfair, he or she can still ask for the case to be heard by an impartial jury.[26]

Rules And Regulations Governing Plea Bargaining

THE ATTORNEY GENERAL'S GUIDELINES AND CBA STANDARDS

The Canadian *Criminal Code* contains no provisions which deal explicitly with the subject of plea negotiations between prosecutorial authorities and the accused or his representatives. One provision which is particularly relevant to this important topic, however, is that of subsection 606(4), which says that:

> Notwithstanding any other provision of this Act, where an accused pleads not guilty of the offense charged but guilty of an included or other offense, the court may in its discretion with the consent of the prosecutor accept such plea of guilty and, if such plea is accepted, shall find the accused not guilty of the offense charged.[27]

While this section of the Code apparently provides a mechanism for plea negotiations, only informal guidelines can be found on the topic. For example, in 1972, just two years after Rule 11(e) was adopted in the United States, the Ontario Attorney General, Dalton Bales, sent a memorandum to all Crown attorneys concerning conduct of plea discussions. In that memorandum, Mr. Bales enumerated certain principles applicable to plea discussions. (Reproduced in Appendix B.) By this action, the Attorney General's office informally established guidelines analogous to the formalized Rule 11 guidelines adopted in the United States. Similarly, in 1974, the Canadian Bar Association Code of Professional Conduct adopted a rule defining the circumstances under which it is proper to advise a client to enter a guilty plea, and cautioning *against* doing so where the principal purpose is for expediency. (See Appendix C.)

In January 1976, the Attorney General in Canada established a Task Force on the administration of justice. Its purpose was to: 1) "examine the existing justice services in Canada; 2) gather data relating to the cost of delivery of these justice services; 3) recommend minimum standards for justice services and the cost implications thereof."[28] In September 1976, the Canadian Criminology and Corrections Association, which was part of the Task Force, noted the need for a Canadian manual of criminal justice standards. Furthermore, the Canadian Criminology and Corrections Association noted that, while standards for criminal justice had been developed in other countries, the degree to which they might be applicable to Canada had not been ascertained. While several criminal justice agencies in Canada had developed sets of standards, none of them had been accepted nationally.

The 1976 report issued by the Canadian Criminology and Corrections Association showed strong disapproval of plea bargaining, apparently recommending its abolition. (Relevant portions are quoted in Appendix E.) Perhaps prompted by the activities of the Canadian Criminology and Correction Association, the Ministry of the Attorney-General sent another memorandum in 1976 to all Crown attorneys, again setting guidelines.[29]

The Canadian Bar Association also has formally recognized the propriety of plea bargaining with the following standards:

IMPLEMENTATION OF A STANDARD RECOGNIZING THE LEGITIMACY OF PLEA BARGAINING AND PROVIDING FOR ITS REGULATION

(a) Regulation by Internal Administrative Control

Province of Ontario has developed a set of guidelines for "plea discussion" -- although they are not as detailed as those who seek to structure prosecutorial decision-making would wish.

(b) Judicial Regulation of the Practice

(i) *abuse of process doctrine*
The only technique presently employed in controlling the exercise of prosecutorial discretion is the doctrine of abuse of process.

(ii) *close scrutiny of the guilty plea*
Where there is abuse in the process, or where the defendant does not fully appreciate his situation, he should be allowed to withdraw his guilty plea. Similarly the trial judge may be placed under a duty to investigate all plea agreements with a view to ascertaining both their fairness to the defendant and their acceptability in terms of the broader interests of society.[30]

The floodgates burst in October of 1990 when the Supreme Court of Canada threw out the case *R. v. Askov*,[31] ruling that delays of longer than eight months were unreasonable. The defendants had been found guilty, but were set free because they had waited 34 months for a trial in Brampton, Ontario. The decision, which rocked the overloaded Ontario judicial system, led to the dismissal or withdrawal of about 50,000 charges, ranging from impaired driving to assault and fraud -- because defendants waited more than eight months for a trial.

The Supreme Court took the unusual step of looking at statistics from other provinces and the U.S. It found the average delays in many Ontario courts of a year or more were above what is reasonable. The Supreme Court said six to eight months is not an absolute ceiling. Complex cases necessarily justify longer delays than simple ones. An accused, noted the court, can also contribute to the delay. But the one thing it said was not an acceptable excuse is lack of court resources, even when budgets are tight. *Askov* shifted the burden of proof from the accused onto the Crown to prove that a delay is not unreasonable.

But in May of 1991, the Ontario Court of Appeal ruled that causes for delays should be reviewed case-by-case when trials take more than eight months to schedule. Ontario chief justice Charles Dubin wrote in *R. V. Reginald Bennett*, one of the six cases, "like Madam Justice Louise Arbour, I do not read the reasons for judgment of the Supreme Court of Canada as prescribed a statutory limitation period which, if exceeded, must result in automatic stays of charges."[32]

The Ontario justices are now saying the limitation period may be different for each case. As a first step, defense counsel trying to have a case thrown out because of delay must prove the delays would be shorter in another comparable jurisdiction.

While the decision has given the lower courts some flexibility, Ontario's lower court judges are split over which decision to follow. The *Askov* ruling has dramatically reduced the backlog in Ontario criminal courts, the wait for a trial date in Toronto, for example, in 1997 was about three months instead of five or six months. Before *Askov* there were no guarantees. The Attorney General's office is in the process of adding judges, crown attorneys and court support staff to handle the load. To increase the number of cases heard each day, some courtrooms have added a 4pm-7pm session on top of the regular round from 10am-3pm. Some courts are also being double booked, so a second set of cases are ready to fill in the slack if court finishes early that day.[33]

The Attorney General of Ontario announced that significant steps toward increasing efficiency and fairness has been taken. According to Marion Boyd, the Ministry will implement increased screening of cases, timely disclosure of the Crown's case to fair, prompt and efficient resolution discussions to resolve criminal cases as soon as possible in the best interests of the victim, the accused and society.

In 1993, the Ontario Ministry of the Attorney General's Advisory Committee on Charge Screening, Disclosure, and Resolution Discussions, chaired by The Honourable G. Arthur Martin, proposed eighty recommendations for the improvement of the criminal justice system in the Province of Ontario.[34] The Martin committee was established following the *Askov* decision, to evaluate pre-trial procedures in the criminal courts. The Committee was chaired by Martin, an eminent jurist with an outstanding reputation in Canada and other countries as a leading member of the defense bar a law teacher and a member of the Ontario Court of Appeal from 1973-1988. It included representation from the defense bar, the crown attorney system, police forces, the federal department of justice and the Ontario Ministry of the Solicitor General.

The Martin Committee was created in June 1991 to analyze ways in which to resolve criminal cases as quickly as possible, while maintaining high standards of fairness in the criminal courts of Ontario.[35] The criminal justice system in Ontario over the previous decade had been strained due to the inability of the system to efficiently dispose of increasing numbers of criminal cases. The growing backlog of cases in Ontario, it was found, was resulting in large numbers of cases being dismissed.[36] The numerous recommendations, most of which were adopted by the Attorney General of Ontario during the 1993/94 fiscal year, were written with input from police, Crown counsel, defense attorneys, and victim and witness groups.[37]

The first set of recommendations of the Martin Committee deals with the charge screening process. The Martin Committee recommended that the "reasonable prospect of conviction" threshold test be adopted for all offenses to prevent the wasting of resources on cases that the prosecution has little chance of winning.[38] In addition, the Martin Committee recommended that an analysis of the admissibility of the evidence be conducted to determine if enough evidence can be presented in court for a "reasonable prospect of conviction."[39] Screening is to take place only at the post-charge stages, as recommended by the Martin Report, so as not to interfere with the traditional independence of the police in deciding whether to lay charges.[40]

A second set of recommendations from the Martin Committee deals with the Crown's obligation to disclose all relevant documents in its possession. The Martin Committee recommended that the police officers should take special care in collecting "accurate and contemporaneous notes during their investigations."[41]

Related measures include pilot testing of programs such as diverting certain criminal offenses from the court system, using community-based alternatives such as compensation or restitution of victims, videotaping of confessions and witness statements, videotaping impaired drivers at the scene or in the police station to reduce time in court, creating fast-track courts to hear impaired-driving cases, and using alternative ways such as mediation to resolve civil cases.

The Martin Committee also recommended that the Attorney General of Ontario issue a new directive to Crown counsel regarding disclosure "to assist in guaranteeing the accused's common law and constitutional rights to a fair trial and to make full answer and defence."[42] According to the report, the directive would be a significant expansion of the existing directive to Crown Attorneys on disclosure and would provide considerable additional details on the Crown's obligation to disclose all relevant information in its possession. The Martin Committee stated that timely and full disclosure by the Crown of all relevant information about a case to the defense results in benefits to the administration of justice in Ontario, among which include:

(a) the resolution of non-contentious and time-consuming issues in advance of the preliminary hearing or the trial, which ensures the most efficient use of court time;

(b) the waiver or shortening of preliminary hearings and the shortening of trials; and

(c) early resolution of cases, including, where appropriate, the entry of pleas of guilty or the withdrawal of charges.[43]

Moreover, the Martin Committee recommended that all decisions by the Crown "not to disclose on grounds of either privilege or relevance [be] reviewable by the trial judge."[44]

The final set of recommendations set forth by the Martin Committee pertains to plea discussions. The Martin Committee stated that resolution discussions (i.e., plea bargaining) "are an essential part of the criminal justice system in Ontario, and, when properly conducted, benefit not only the accused, but also victims, witnesses, counsel, and the administration of justice generally."[45] The Martin Committee recommended: "that Crown counsel should not accept a plea of guilty to a charge where he or she knows that the accused is innocent";[46] "where Crown counsel knows that the prosecution will never be able to prove a material element of the case, Crown counsel has a duty to disclose this to the defence";[47] "that the Attorney General should require his or her agents conducting resolution discussions to consider the interests of victims";[48] and, "as a general rule, counsel must honour all agreements reached after resolution discussions."[49] Finally, the Martin Committee stated "that a judge presiding at a pre-hearing conference should not be involved in plea bargaining. . . [except], however, in resolving the issue of sentence by expressing an opinion as to whether a proposed sentence is too high, too low, or within an appropriate range",[50] and that "it is inappropriate to engage in resolution discussions with the trial judge in Chambers."[51] To date, the Martin Committee Report is one of the first and most thorough set of recommendations governing plea negotiation in Canada.

PLEA BARGAINING RULES AND PROCEDURES AS SEEN IN CASE LAW

There are very few cases in which Canadian courts have expressed a view as to the merits or propriety of prosecutorial plea bargaining or have hinted at plea bargaining in any way. An analysis of the cases appears to reveal a distinction between agreements reached before plea and agreements reached after plea. The so-called joint submission (joint recommendation of sentence by Crown and defense), which will be discussed later in this section, can be the result of an agreement reached either before or after the plea has been entered.

The case of *R. v. Agozzino* (1970),[52] (described in the endnotes) appears to be a classic example of the plea bargain between the prosecution and the defense which was later repudiated by the Crown on appeal. The Ontario Court of Appeals does not study or pronounce upon the sensibility or propriety of plea bargaining, but confines itself to determining a proper result upon being faced with that circumstance. Its decision in favor of the accused is predicated upon avoiding unfairness "not only to the Magistrate but to the accused." This appears to be an application of the principle of detrimental reliance found in the law of contracts.[53]

The English case of *Frank Richard Turner* (1970)[54] is a landmark decision both for England and Canada. On January 26, 1970 at North-East London Quarter Sessions, Mr. Turner pleaded not guilty to the theft of a car. On January 27, 1970 he retracted that plea of not guilty and pleaded guilty, whereupon a formal verdict was taken from the jury and he was fined £50, with four months imprisonment in default of payment within four months, his license was endorsed, and he was ordered to pay £75 towards the costs of the prosecution. The accused appealed against his conviction, alleging that he did not have the opportunity to retract his plea of not guilty freely, and that his mind was not with his plea of not guilty and pleading guilty, and that, as it were, his mind did not go with the plea of guilty. The Criminal Court of Appeals therefore had to determine whether the prisoner in the circumstances had a free choice.

While the trial was still in progress, the defense Counsel advised his client to seriously reconsider his plea and change his plea of not guilty to a guilty plea. During the course of the trial the defense Counsel was consulting with the deputy Chairman. The Court found no fault with Counsel's action to advise his client in strong terms so long as he had made it clear that the ultimate decision was with the client. The accused still chose to proceed with the case. However, just prior to recommending the proceedings, the Clerk of the Court conveyed to defense Counsel that the judge would not allow more time. Although that the accused had been warned that the final decision was his, once he felt that this was an intimation from the judge, it was unrealistic to think that he really had a free choice. Thus, the Court allowed the appeal, treating the plea as a nullity, declaring a mistrial and advising a new proceeding.

The Court of Criminal Appeal of England concluded its opinion with a practice direction to trial judges and counsel on what it described as "the vexed question of so-called 'plea bargaining.'" The court began with a description of the duty of defense counsel:

> Counsel must be completely free to do what is his duty, namely to give the accused the best advice he can and if need be, advice in strong terms. This will often include advice that a plea of guilty, showing an element of remorse, is a mitigating factor which may well enable the Court to give a lesser sentence than would otherwise be the case. Counsel, of course, will emphasize that the accused must not plead guilty unless he has committed the acts constituting the offence charged.

The accused, having considered counsel's advice, must have a complete freedom of choice whether to plead guilty or not guilty.[55]

The Court of Criminal Appeal then proceeded to describe proper protocol for involving the trial judge in any plea discussions:

> There must be freedom of access between counsel and judge. Any discussion, however, which takes place must be between the judge and both counsel for the defense and counsel for the prosecution. If a solicitor representing the accused is in the Court, he should be allowed to attend the discussion, if he so desires.
>
> This freedom of access is important because there may be matters calling for communication or discussion, which are of such a nature that counsel cannot in the interests of his client mention them in open court. Purely by way of example, counsel for the defense may by way of mitigation wish to tell the judge that the accused has not long to live, is suffering maybe from cancer, of which he is and should remain ignorant.

Again, counsel on both sides may wish to discuss with the judge whether it would be proper, in a particular case, for the prosecution to accept a plea to a lesser offence.

It is of course imperative that so far as possible justice might be administered in open Court. Counsel should, therefore, only ask to see the judge when it is felt to be really necessary and the judge must be careful only to treat such communications as private where, in fairness to the accused person, this is necessary.[56]

Next, the Court of Criminal Appeal quite clearly stated the limits imposed on the involvement by the trial judge:

The judge should, subject to the one exception referred to hereafter, never indicate the sentence which he is minded to impose. A statement that on a plea of guilty he would impose one sentence but that on a conviction following a plea of not guilty he would impose a severer sentence is one which should never be made. This could be taken to be undue pressure on the accused, thus depriving him of that complete freedom of choice which is essential. Such cases, however, are in the experience of the Court happily rare. What on occasions does appear to happen however is that a judge will tell counsel that, having read the depositions and the antecedents, he can safely say that on a plea of guilty he will for instance make a probation order, something which may be helpful to counsel in advising the accused. The judge in such a case is no doubt careful not to mention what he would do if the accused were convicted following a plea of not guilty. Even so, the accused may well get the impression that the judge is intimating that in that event a severer sentence, maybe a custodial sentence, would result, so that again he may feel under pressure. This accordingly must also not be done.

The only exception to this rule is that it should be permissible for a judge to say, if it be the case, that whatever happens, whether the accused pleads guilty or not guilty, the sentence will or will not take a particular form, e.g. a probation order or a fine or a custodial sentence. (This is what the Clerk testified he told counsel, but the Court found he was wrong in his recollection.)

> Finally, where any such discussion on sentence has taken place between judge and counsel, counsel for the defense should disclose this to the accused and inform him of what took place.[57]

Without dealing generally with the acceptability of plea bargaining, the court of criminal appeal in England clearly condemned involvement by third judges except to a very limited extent. Counsel are enjoined to emphasize that the accused must not plead guilty unless he has committed the acts constituting the offense charged, and it is mandatory that the accused, having considered counsel's advice, have complete freedom of choice and feel no pressure whether to plead guilty or not guilty.

In *R. v. Brown* (1972),[58] once again (as in *Agozzino*, above) the Ontario Court of Appeals was confronted with the repudiation by the Crown at trial of its plea bargain agreement with the defense. Although the court did not mention *Agozzino*, the judge followed a consistent line in holding the Crown to its bargain. Again the court neglected to comment more generally on plea bargaining procedures but simply noted its existence in this case -- and dealt with it by applying the principle of detrimental reliance.

The Quebec Court of Appeals in *Attorney General of Canada v. Roy* (1972)[59] again clearly applied the principle of detrimental reliance in recognizing that the accused may have predicated his plea upon the sentence position to be adopted by the Crown. In connection with this case the court said:

> The Crown, like any other litigant, ought not to be heard to repudiate before an appellate court the position taken by its counsel in the trial court, except for the gravest possible reasons. Such reasons might be where the sentence was an illegal one, or where the Crown can demonstrate that its counsel had in some way been misled, or finally, where it can be shown that the public interest in the orderly administration of justice is outweighed by the gravity of the crime and the gross insufficiency of the sentence.

In *R. v. Wood* (1975),[60] the Alberta Court of Appeals emphatically denounced judicial involvement of any kind in plea bargaining. Without expressly asserting whether or not there ought to be plea bargain agreements, the decision highlighted the difficulties that may be present where an appeal is taken. Judge McDermid considered whether Crown counsel had been right to say he had no objection to the provincial court judge taking part in a private discussion concerning sentence prior to a plea being taken. In other words, should a judge take part in "plea bargaining"? The answer was unequivocally negative, noting *Turner* and observing that "there is no place in the sentencing procedure for hole-and-corner bargaining," and further stating "to take part in a discussion of sentencing prior to a plea being taken would constitute a grave dereliction of duty." The agent of the Attorney General told defense counsel that he would not seek a jail sentence if the accused entered a guilty plea. Clearly, the effect of that intimation would be to encourage the accused to plead guilty."[61]

In *Perkins & Pigeau v. The Queen* (1976),[62] the Quebec Court of Appeals was obviously affronted by the hypocrisy, to which the Crown and defense were trying to make it a party, in prosecuting for the offense of possession for the purpose of trafficking, but regarding it for sentencing as the offense of illegal importing. The court stated:

> Either the accused was guilty and must face the mandatory sentence imposed by law or he was innocent and must be acquitted. A plea to a lesser offense may be accepted if the Crown doubts its ability to prove a charge, but that was not the case here since the Crown attorney admitted having enough evidence to establish importing.

Although it may be argued that this is an extraordinary situation, the concept of prosecuting according to the offense substantiated by the evidence finds support in this decision, at least insofar as it repudiates the divorce of the law from reality which often result with plea bargaining in which the parties agree to treat the criminal conduct as something other than what it really is according to law.

The decision of *Regina v. Roy* (1976),[63] in line with *Turner* and *Wood*, clearly rejects judicial involvement in plea bargaining, at least as far as the presiding judge is concerned. The opinion of the Ontario Court of Appeals suggests that this prohibition would extend to a jury case as well since any preconceptions a judge might form in negotiations could be reflected in his charge to the jury or sentence upon a conviction.

In *Her Majesty The Queen v. Daniel Charles Talbot* (1976)[64] the Crown made a plea bargain with the participation of the judge, to which the Ontario Court of Appeals apparently applied U.S. criteria such as voluntariness, knowledge, adhesion by the parties, and publicity. Query the propriety of such a discussion with the judge in view of the English *Turner*-line of authorities.

In *Regina v. Arthur* (1978),[65] again the principle of detrimental reliance was invoked for the protection of the accused. The accused pleaded guilty to a charge of causing bodily harm by criminal negligence after the Crown had agreed not to speak to sentencing if that occurred. Then, when the trial judge asked Crown counsel if he opposed the defense request for a suspended sentence, he replied that he had made "certain undertakings" and had "no comment." The Crown appealed from the suspended sentence and 3 years probation that was imposed. Although the Crown sought to qualify the foregoing circumstances by claiming the agreement did not apply to any appeal the Crown might take, the judge he said that "in any event, to give weight to the Crown's contention that the agreement would not apply to an appeal would, for all intent and purpose, make it worthless." Without critical analysis of the propriety of the plea bargaining in general, the Prince Edward Island Court of Appeals continues to intimate but not express its disapproval of the practice.

Finally, in *Regina v. Ferrio & Richards* (1979),[66] the language employed by the Ontario Court of Appeals in censuring the Crown for repudiating its plea agreement is inconsistent with a finding that it had probably been simply forgotten. Again, this reflects a silent acceptance of the practice of plea negotiation.

As the preceding cases illustrate, the most significant developments in the area of plea discussions in Canada took place after 1970. It may be that the landmark developments in the United States which occurred around 1971, particularly the *Santobello* decision and the adoption of Rule 11(e), provided impetus to take a closer look at the practice in Canada.

An interesting aspect of these cases is the way in which they dealt with the very existence of plea bargaining. Unlike the *Santobello* decision in the United States and the subsequent adoption of Rule 11, both of which provide a clear stamp of approval on the practice, the above decisions seem to avoid any such endorsement. These cases give the impression that the Canadian courts have reluctantly dealt with the legal entanglements that arise in plea bargaining but seem, at the same time, to be leaving open the question of whether the practice should be used or not. In any event, they are very clear that the judge may *not* participate or hint at any leniency simply to encourage a plea for the sake of expedience. As we will see later, it may be the general suspicion of plea bargaining that generates a safeguard against abuses even in the absence of the formal rules and constraints enforced in the United States.

HYBRID JUDICIAL PLEA BARGAINING

Canadian courts also practice what is referred to as "hybrid judicial plea bargaining." This typically involves a pretrial meeting of the Crown, defense and a judge (*other than* the judge who will conduct the trial) in the course of which a discussion of disposition, including sentence, occurs. Explicit or implicit, the purpose of the discussion is to ascertain the sentence position to which the Crown will commit itself and of which the court would approve in the event of a guilty plea. The judge, who will *not* be involved in the trial, will commonly volunteer his opinion as to the sentence he would impose in the event of a trial following a plea of not guilty, as compared to the lesser sentence that might be expected were a plea of guilty to be entered and a corresponding degree of remorse demonstrated. Likewise, the pretrial judge will often participate in discussions involving other means of extending leniency to the accused in return for an admission of guilty, such as a reduction of charges and the kind of sentences. Characteristically in this regime, the discussion is to be "off-the-record" and the pretrial judge is not to be the trial judge or communicate to him the contents of the discussion. This practice is said to enable the judiciary to play a role in plea bargaining while avoiding the worst of its disadvantages. The two crucial premises of this practice are (1) the separation of the pretrial judge and the trial judge, and (2) the preservation of the discretion of the trial judge.[67] This is significantly different than the practice in the United States where the trial judge is often the same person as the pretrial judge, as previously discussed in Chapter 2.

JOINT SUBMISSIONS

The term "joint submission" refers to a process where both sides (Crown and defense) present to the court a guilty plea and make a joint recommendation as to the appropriate sentence. The Cases involving this practice demonstrate the attitudes of judges and courts in general toward joint submissions. In some instances, the courts have adopted the recommendation and, in other instances, they have not. On occasion their position is ambiguous.

In *Regina v. Johnston & Tremayne* (1970)[68] it appears that the Ontario Court of Appeals treated as inconsequential on appeal the Crown's more lenient position in a joint submission to the trial judge. While the appellate court decided to reduce the imposed sentences, it did so for other reasons unrelated to the joint submission.

In *Regina v. Greene* (1971),[69] Judge Graburn of the Ontario Court of Appeals made certain oral remarks, addressed to counsel at large as well as those present, following a sentence in which he adopted the joint submission recommendation. In those remarks, Judge Graburn welcomed submissions made by counsel when a consensus could be agreed upon a sentence, and reiterated the court's intention to give effect to those submissions unless they should be contrary to principle or unreasonable on their face. He emphasized three points. First, the basis of such recommendations must be thorough and the result of a careful investigation of the circumstances by counsel. Secondly, the recommendations must be in accordance with legal principle and, on their face, reasonable. Thirdly, it is proper and desirable that the form of sentence, if it can be agreed upon, be suggested, but only in the most unusual cases ought the quantum of sentence be suggested since that is in the absolute jurisdiction of the court.

These remarks were evidently intended to qualify certain things Judge Graburn said "in another place"[70] as he put it, and perhaps to be regarded as a practice direction, as far as his own court was concerned, at least, in view of his request to the Crown counsel to relate them to members of the Crown attorney's staff.

These cases show clear approval of "joint submissions" but do not necessarily contemplate their having been agreed upon before the plea was entered. Obviously, however, guilty pleas nearly always are by joint submissions, whether or not previously commented on by the pretrial judge. In all cases, the trial judge retains complete discretion to accept or reject the joint submission.

In *Her Majesty The Queen v. Kirkpatrick* (1971),[71] the Quebec Court of Appeals seems to adopt a similar approach to that in *Johnston & Tremayne* although here it was a Crown appeal. The dissenting opinion referred to *Agozzino* but does not address the effect of the distinction between an agreement made before plea between the Crown and the defense (*Agozzino*), and the mere submission by the Crown of a sentence without such an agreement, as here.

The case of *Regina v. Pretty* (1971),[72] represents an example of a joint submission ignored by both the trial judge and the Prince Edward Island Court of Appeals. The magistrate's report on sentencing hinted at the possibility of arrangements between the Crown and the accused, but the report of the decision fails to substantiate that fact. Interestingly enough, that merely caused the trial judge to temper his sentence, not slavishly follow the joint submission.

In *Regina v. Fleury* (1971),[73] unlike *Kirkpatrick* and *Mouffe*, the Quebec Court of Appeals held the Crown to its position at trial, possibly extending, in effect, the principle of detrimental reliance to the trial judge having regard to the submissions made to him by the Crown. The court was not satisfied that the circumstances warranted a repudiation by the Crown of its former position.

In *Regina v. Cusack* (1978),[74] the Nova Scotia Court of Appeals clearly recognized the difference between plea agreements between the Crown and defense to which the concept of detrimental reliance would apply, and unconditional guilty pleas where the concept does not apply. In the latter situation where the Crown makes submissions that are accepted by the trial judge in sentencing, the appeal court may tend to treat it merely as a question of the relationship between the Crown and the judge, with little reliance entitled to placed on the Crown's position. Regrettably, the Nova Scotia court again (expressly) avoided pronouncing upon the propriety of "plea bargaining," but merely described the more binding consequences it entails for the Crown.

Regina v. Joseph Lapointe (1978)[75] is an example of the joint submission type of case, which, as noted already, does not necessarily imply a plea agreement between the Crown and defense. The Ontario Court of Appeals here simply demonstrates that such a submission ought to be accorded substantial weight.

To summarize, the significance of these cases is that they demonstrate a certain concern for ensuring that the sentence fits the crime. That decision is reserved to the judge and, as these cases show, the judges exercise that authority.

JUSTIFICATION AND CRITICISMS OF PLEA BARGAINING

Much criticism has been leveled in Ontario at the concept of plea discussions and agreements. Even more has been directed toward the way in which the discussions are conducted and the agreements concluded, especially on the lack of uniform practices.

There are those in the Ontario Law Reform Commission who are strongly opposed to plea bargaining. In a report published in 1973 by this Commission, it was admitted that "It is not a recent phenomenon, but . . . has been exacerbated by an infiltration from the United States of what we regard as an unhealthy philosophy quite alien to our concept of an open, fair and public administration of justice."[76] This accusation is quite interesting from a country whose archives indicate a long history of plea bargaining, as will be shown in later chapters. The Commission goes on to say that plea bargaining exists because of the necessity of "disposing of a volume of cases without lengthy delays,"[77] and then launches into a more detailed description of the process.

The conclusions which this Ontario Law Reform Commission reached in 1973 were substantially the same as those arrived at by the National Advisory Commission for Criminal Justice Standards and Goals in the United States, although the Ontario Commission hastened to point out that "our conclusions were arrived at and recorded before the publication of the National Advisory Commission's standard."[78] The Ontario Commission proceeded on the principles that "the conviction of an accused person should depend not on negotiation but on the evidence available to convict him and the sentence imposed should depend on the action which best serves rehabilitative and deterrent needs."[79] The Commission was quite blunt in stating its recommendations:

> As soon as possible, but in no event later than 1978, negotiations between defendants and their attorneys and prosecutors concerning concessions to be made in return for guilty pleas ***should be abolished.*** In the event that the prosecution makes a recommendation as to sentence, it should not be affected by the willingness of the defendant to plead guilty to some or all of the offenses with which he is charged. A plea of guilty should not be considered by the court in determining the sentence to be imposed [emphasis added].[80]

While the Law Reform Commission set a 1978 deadline for the total abolition of plea bargaining, Justice Arthur Martin of the Ontario Court of Appeals believes that plea negotiations are a way of life. Justice Martin, who has been on the Court of Appeals for decades, admits that plea negotiations, although not spoken of in public, have gone on for a long time, increasingly so with new rules of disclosure. Fifty years ago, Crown attorneys were required to disclose very little to the accused, but there has been a legal obligation for the Crown to disclose much more in recent years. This, added to the growing number of lawyers, make these discussions inevitable.[81] These discussions are "perfectly proper" in his opinion as long as they are conducted in good faith. Justice Martin further states that he sees:

> nothing inherently wrong in defense counsel and Crown counsel speaking to the judge, outlining the facts to him, if it is a case where his approval is required for a plea of guilty to a lesser offence, to canvass his attitude and . . . [he sees] nothing wrong in the Crown indicating to the judge what the Crown's attitude is with respect to sentence.[82]

The judge, in Justice Martin's opinion, can properly indicate whether the Crown's view as to sentence seems reasonable or unacceptable, "but he never binds himself as to what sentence he will impose."[83] The judge must always be free to change his mind, also in good faith, if there is evidence in the case which is presented which convinces him that this is the right thing to do.

Justice Martin, a conservative who is widely respected in Ontario legal circles, may believe that a conscientious judge can keep plea negotiations from usurping the role of the court. The Law Reform Commission, however, is quite worried about the abuses which it claims to be inherent in the practice. According to the Commission, a false impression can be created in the mind of the accused as to the extent of the influence of the prosecutor in securing a specific sentence. The existence of the practice can lead to an expectation by the accused that a "deal" will be offered and, if none is made, he can use delaying tactics such as dismissing his counsel on the eve of the trial, in the hopes of exerting pressure on the prosecutor to offer a concession.[84]

Negotiations are not done under public scrutiny, but usually in a Crown office. Some people may be left with the impression that justice is buyable or, if not buyable, then it is dispensed according to friendship or some other improper motive. It is argued that, if bargaining and negotiations are to become a way of life in Canada, then the Crown will be sorely tempted to overcharge so that they will be in a better position to negotiate.[85] This already is a problem in the United States where prosecutors have been accused of overcharging in order to force the defendant to plead guilty.

The editor of *Chitty's Law Journal* wrote in 1978, defending the concept of plea bargaining that, "if properly managed, [it] can work for the benefit of anyone. There is no need to eliminate the plea bargaining process just because of the occasional danger of mismanagement."[86] One of the problems he saw was in the term itself, where the word "bargain" connotes a haggle in a marketplace descending into the courtroom.

> In an absolutist regime where everything is obviously and clearly black and white to those who hold power, the negotiated plea has no place at

all. In a democratic community, it should not be eliminated. It is like our economy. We know that it cannot operate in perfect balance and compromises have to be made.[87]

The effects of plea negotiations in Canada, real or merely imagined, are important enough to have excited considerable controversy within the profession and amongst the public at large, sometimes promoted by the press. For example, on December 13, 1971 the *Toronto Globe & Mail* and the *Ottawa Citizen* newspapers carried sensational front page stories of the sudden conclusion of the trial of 13 inmates of Kingston Penitentiary for murder. They had entered pleas of guilty to the lesser offenses of manslaughter or of assault, and the press claimed that there had been secret deals in which the trial judge had helped to negotiate in his chambers the settlement that occurred, including agreements on the length of the sentences to be imposed. The trial judge emphatically denied that he had participated in any plea bargaining, and in fact the matter was somewhat more moderately treated in subsequent issues of the newspaper. The *Globe & Mail* eventually claimed that plea bargaining was simply a symptom of the legal profession's own self-protection.[88]

As mentioned above, the Law Reform Commission of Ontario in 1973 adopted a hostile position towards plea bargaining. In particular, it sharply criticized the argument that plea bargaining is necessary and justifiable as a means of reducing the backlog of cases clogging the criminal courts. In the Commission's view, to engage in such a practice will inevitably "destroy confidence in the courts and create distrust and suspicion of favors." The real ligaments that hold society together, according to the Commission, are to be found in the fair, just and open procedures of the Courts.[89] In line with these sentiments has been an increasingly marked trend in the Canadian Courts to denounce the practice of plea bargaining as being improper.[90] While plea negotiations are a fact of life in the Canadian criminal justice system, it has been the subject of considerable controversy over the past twenty-five years.

VIEWS AND OBSERVATIONS ON THE ROLE OF THE CROWN

In contrast to the United States, where prosecutors are elected on a partisan basis for a four-year term, Crown attorneys are appointed members of the court. It has been a long tradition as well as an established principle that the decision whether or not to prosecute is a matter that is decided apart from the public or political pressures. Further, in determining whether the prosecution should take place or not, the Crown considers the interest of society as a whole. As one Crown attorney commented:

> We are not responsible in the way that district attorneys are. We are not elected; we are not hired or fired by the electorate, with whatever ramifications may flow from that in terms of plea bargaining that we carry on. You're more likely to get into trouble by plea bargaining than you are to be criticized for taking a trial and losing. You will be criticized for taking it and plea bargaining that case and settling for a charge that the victim or the public sees as not serious enough.[91]

A motivating factor for Crown's bargaining is evidence of harshness of conviction or sentence. That is, Crown counsel may usurp the role of the judge by plea bargaining if they think the accused is likely to get a harsher sentence than they think he deserves. However the Canadian criminal law has very few mandatory, minimum sentences. As a result, there is less incentive to bargain for this purpose then in the United States. A Crown attorney can always avoid harshness without plea bargaining, a charge can be reduced without requiring the accused to plead guilty.[92] A senior prosecutor suggested that "true" bargaining -- in the sense of Crown and defense counsel discussing the plea and sentence with the trial judge -- does not exist in Canada.[93]

In actual practice, according to Sarah Welch, a Provincial Crown Attorney in Toronto, the accused who pleads guilty in Canada often gets the same sentence which he would have received had the case gone to trial and resulted in a conviction. She indicated, and her sentiments were echoed by Michael Dambrot, Head Crown Attorney, that the charges would in no case be reduced to less than those which were fairly indicated by the criminal activity, and the main benefit of plea negotiations was that the accused would know in advance what to expect in court and be spared the worry of uncertainty.[94]

In Canada there is a preliminary inquiry which allows the accused to clarify his plea. The accused is informed by his attorney whether or not the Crown has a sufficient case to prove guilt beyond a reasonable doubt at trial. If the accused is led to believe that the Crown's case is this sound, it is reasonable to assume that he would opt for a plea of guilty. By doing this, he would perhaps gain a lighter sentence or ease the financial burden of a contested trial.[95] According to Head Crown Attorney Dambrot, there are also discussions between the lawyers for the Crown and the defense on a more formal basis. In his dominion level office there is:

> a standardized, at least a principled approach, to work that people are expected to pursue. For example, when anyone discusses a file with a defense lawyer and there is a discussion about some way of resolving the case, and something is offered and accepted or offered and refused, everyone is expected to record that on the file and that becomes binding on anyone else who deals with the file. At least it's *prima facie* binding. And in order to depart from what was said on an earlier occasion by another prosecutor requires the subsequent prosecutor either to go back to the first person and explain why he wants to vary the position or . . . to come to me to resolve it.[96]

Provincial Crown Attorney Welch commented that, in her experience, "99.9% of the time all of these bargains are simply verbal agreements. Nobody ever writes them out or sends confirming letters."[97] This is quite different from some courts in the United States which provide forms on which the details of the bargain are set down and the document is signed by the accused, who affirms that he knows of his right to a trial and, in light of the agreement, is not demanding that right.

Another Crown attorney commented that there was nothing improper about counsel suggesting an appropriate range of sentence to the judge -- e.g., a representation to the effect that "this offense does not merit penitentiary time." However, the judicial participants have objected to this practice on the basis that it impinged upon their discretion as to sentencing.[98]

A senior Crown attorney describes her experience with plea bargaining in the United States:

> I had a man charged with rape, assault, bodily harm and various other things and he fled the jurisdiction and ended up down in the States. He was picked up in Carolina, I believe, and he committed a very serious robbery case and was charged along with that with attempted murder, and they knew that we wanted him back in Toronto for trial, and he entered into a plea bargaining contract, really. It was all written out and it was in consideration -- you'd never get this in Canada, a document actually drawn up -- that in consideration of the district attorney offering me such and such, I hereby agree to plead guilty and I am only pleading guilty on the explicit understanding that I will receive a sentence of no more than such and such. And in fact he got a sentence that you wouldn't have, nobody here would plea bargain. The attempted murder was dropped, the robbery -- it was a six month sentence but effectively suspended. So that what happened . . . . My impression, and I don't

know if it's accurate or not, is that there are certain plea bargains in the States that would not be sanctioned here. . . . [Y]ou have the impression that because the district attorney is elected, not appointed, that there's far greater concern for your track record in the United States and in your conviction rate, and therefore on a case that is borderline, a tough case that's a serious offense but you may not get a conviction, I think there's the tendency here to go to trial rather than reduce the charge. . . . [I]t's my impression that in the States there might be a greater tendency to reduce the charge for the security of the conviction.[99]

VIEWS AND OBSERVATIONS ON THE ROLE OF THE DEFENSE ATTORNEY

For the defense counsel, it has been suggested that a clear advantage of the negotiated guilty plea over a trial is that the former permits the busy practitioner to deal quickly and efficiently with a much larger caseload. However, two Canadian commentators have pointed out, "[t]he possibility that defense counsel might feel pleased with such a procedure . . . is irrelevant; criminal procedures are not created for the benefit of lawyers!"[100] "The 'advantages' of quick fees and expeditious case flow to defense counsel are surely outweighed by the existence of a market system which may actively encourage impatient counsel to work in conflict with his duty to clients in obtaining a fair trial wherever matters of fact are in some doubt."[101]

In response to a question about the need for the promulgation of a set of guidelines concerning plea bargaining, a criminal defense attorney commented on the changes that he would like to see:

I think most defense lawyers and Crown attorneys are not concerned about plea bargaining. They consider it right and just, and the only thing they might be concerned about is they would like there to be perhaps a more formal mechanism. To put into our statutes something like there is in the United States, where everyone knows what their role is, what the judge can do, if he doesn't accept it, what the accused can do. I think a lot of people would like a little more certainty under the system. It would be a lot easier to work that way, to attach it to some pretrial hearing to narrow down the issues of the trial.[102]

VIEWS AND OBSERVATIONS ON THE ROLE OF THE JUDGE

In contrast to election of judges in much of the United States, at the provincial judiciary level in Canada the Governor General appoints judges selected by the majority party to the superior court districts in each province for both criminal and civil courts.[103] Canadian judges are not dependent on their public popularity for their jobs and need not be so concerned about the popularity of the decisions they make.[104]

As previously mentioned, judicial participation in plea bargaining is supposed to occur only in a very narrowly confined manner in the Canadian court system. All the judges interviewed stressed that the term "plea negotiations" was more appropriate for the activities. With respect to setting standards for the practice of plea bargaining in Canada, a chief district judge in Ontario pointed out that some standards already existed -- e.g., the ethical standard that defense counsel should not allow a client to plead guilty to an offense where the client appears to be not guilty.[105]

Although acceptance of a guilty plea by the accused to an included or other offense requires the prosecutor's consent, the discretion as to whether such plea will be accepted ultimately resides with the judge. In addition, the accused may only plead guilty to an included or other offense of which, in the determination of the judge, he could be convicted upon indictment before the court. However, it has further been determined[106] by the Supreme Court of Canada that a trial judge is not bound, as a matter of law, to conduct an inquiry into the propriety of a guilty plea which has been entered by the accused.[107] The judge is somewhat dependant in plea bargain situations, therefore, upon the proper and efficient functioning of the other parts of the criminal justice system. In some cases, however, the very fact that the judge has the choice of whether or not to accept a plea of guilty necessarily implies that he will not do so unless he is "sufficiently" informed of the facts upon which the defendant pleads guilty, especially when the charge carries a heavy maximum sentence or the defendant might have good grounds for defense. In some cases, in fact, the courts have reversed convictions based on guilty pleas when the defendant has a good defense in law to the charges and the Crown's contentions could not demolish his defense.[108]

A vast majority of Canadian judges interviewed for the purpose of this book would consider involvement in a plea negotiation as clearly unethical. As previously mentioned, since the Crown can never tie the hands of the trial judge, the Crown is not in a position to ensure that promises made to the accused will ultimately be "delivered". Therefore, it is perhaps inaccurate to refer to agreements between the Crown and defense counsel as "bargain." While the trial judge may, for example, be prepared to go along with the Crown's sentencing recommendations in some cases, there is no guarantee that this will happen in any particular case. Given these factors, which militate against the enforceability of a good number of the types of promises made by the Crown, a number of commentators have started to use such terms as "plea discussions," "plea agreements" or "plea negotiations," instead of the term "plea bargains,"[109] as previously mentioned. It may be that many of those who reject the practice of "plea bargaining" would nevertheless be willing to accept the notion of "plea discussion" (i.e., the courts of appeal in at least two provinces have recently endorsed the view that Crown and defense counsel may advance a joint submission as to sentence, provided it is accepted that such submission does not bind the Court).[110] As one judge stated in *R. v. Simoneau* (1978):[111] "In my view, it is not objectionable for a properly arrived at joint submission to be made nor, where the circumstances call for it, is it objectionable to recommend a specific term, subject always to the overriding discretion of the Court to accept or reject any recommendation."[112]

* * *

In conclusion, as the materials in this section demonstrate, the Canadian attitude toward plea bargaining is cautious. Some sources suggest there should be no plea bargaining. All authorities insist that the trial judge not participate in or initiate plea negotiations. Nonetheless, courts are prepared to listen to joint submissions of proposed plea agreements and the Crown, on occasion, has been held to the recommendation in its joint submission as though the accused had relied on it when agreeing to plead guilty.[113]

Courts in the United States are more openly accepting of the practice of plea bargaining, leading to a more formalized and institutionalized practice there. Canadian courts have fewer formal rules and legal constraints and the practice has not become as thoroughly institutionalized. However, there appear to be certain safeguards inherent in the caution and suspicion with which the practice is treated in Canada.

NOTES

1. Packer, *Criminal Sanction*, 173.
2. *See* Vincent M. Del Buono, ed., *Criminal Procedure in Canada* (Toronto: Butterworths, 1982).
3. J. Hogarth, *Sentencing as a Human Process* (Toronto: University of Toronto Press, 1971), 192.
4. Michael Dambrot, Head Crown Attorney at the time of the interview, interview by author, tape recording, Toronto, Ontario, March 10, 1987. As of 1997, Mr. Dambrot is serving as a judge on the Provincial Court of Ontario. *See also* Craig L. Boydell and Ingrid A. Connidis, ed., *The Canadian Criminal Justice System* (Toronto: Holt, Rinehart and Winston of Canada, 1982).

5. Marc Rosenberg, Criminal Attorney, Greenspan & Rosenberg, and Professor of Law at the time, Osgoode Hall Society School of Law, interview by author, tape recording, Toronto, Ontario, March 11, 1987. As of 1997, Mr. Rosenberg is an appellate judge on the Ontario Court of Appeals.

6. Justice Cou, District Court Judge at the time of the interview, interview by author, Toronto, Ontario, June 1989; Judge Paul LeSage, interview by author, Toronto, Ontario, March 11, 1987.

7. Robert Harvie and Hamar Foster, "Ties That Bind?: The Supreme Court of Canada, American Jurisprudence, and the Revision of Canadian Criminal Law Under the Charter," *Osgoode Hall Law Journal* 28 (1990): 734-735.

8. David M. Paciocco, "The Judicial Repeal of s. 24(2) and the Development of the Canadian Exclusionary Rule," *Criminal Law Quarterly* 32 (1990): 327.

9. Peter W. Hogg, "Canada's New Charter of Rights," *The American Journal of Comparative Law* 32 (1984): 283.

10. Ibid.

11. Ibid.

12. W. Tarnopolsky, "The Historical and Constitutional Context of the Proposed Canadian Charter of Rights and Freedoms," *Law and Contemporary Problems* 44 (1981): 170.

13. Frederick L. Morton, *Law, Politics and the Judicial Process in Canada* (Calgary: University of Calgary Press, 1992), 396.

14. Tarnopolsky, "Historical and Constitutional Context," 173.

15. Robert A. Sedler, "Constitutional Protection of Individual Rights in Canada: The Impact of the New Canadian Charter of Rights and Freedoms," *Notre Dame Law Review* 59 (1984): 1193.

16. Ibid.

17. Hogg, "Canada's New Charter of Rights," 287.

18. Morton, *Law, Politics and the Judicial Process*, 399-400.

19. Seymour Martin Lipset, *Continental Divide: The Values and Institutions of the United States and Canada* (New York: Routledge, Chapman and Hall, 1990), 3.

20. The primary exception to the broad use of the English common law system in Canada is the Province of Quebec which uses the civil law system transferred to Quebec by French settlers in the 1600s and 1700s.

21. Harvie and Foster, "Ties That Bind?," 734.

22. S. Glover, "Exclusion of Evidence: Exclusion of Illegally Obtained Evidence From the Prosecution's Case-in-Chief Under the Canadian Charter of Rights and Freedoms," *Canadian-American Law Journal* 4 (1988): 57-81.

23. Ontario Ministry of the Attorney General, *Report of the Attorney General's Advisory Committee on Charge Screening, Disclosure, and Resolution Discussions* (Toronto: Queen's Printer for Ontario, 1993), 286 [hereinafter referred to as the "Martin Committee Report"].

24. Ibid.

25. Section 11(d) of the Charter states that anyone charged with an offense has the right to "a fair and public hearing by an independent and impartial tribunal."

26. Ontario Ministry of the Attorney General, *Attorney General's Advisory Committee*, 287.

27. *Tremeear's Criminal Code*, the 1997 Annotated (Ontario: Carswell Publishing, 1997).

28. D. F. Cousineau, *Setting Standards for Canadian Criminal Courts: The Case of Plea Bargaining* (Barnaby, British Columbia: Simon Fraser University Press, 1977), 1.

29. Reproduced in Appendix D.

30. Cousineau, *Setting Standards*, 3-4.

31. *Regina v. Askov, et al.*, 59 C.C.C. 3d 449, (1990).

32. *R. v. Reginald Bennett*, 3 O.R. (3d), 193 (1991).

33. Michael Innes, Chief Provincial Crown Attorney, interview by author, February, 1997.

34. Ontario Ministry of the Attorney General, *Attorney General's Advisory Committee.*

35. *Attorney General's Advisory Committee*, 16-17.

36. Ibid., 16-17.

37. Ibid., 1-4.

38. Ibid., 65. The "reasonable prospect of conviction" test, according to the Martin Committee, utilizes a standard which "is higher than that of a *prima facie* case, but . . . *it does not require a conclusion that a conviction be more likely than not.*" Ibid.

39. Ibid.

40. Canada News Wire, December 8, 1993.

41. *Attorney General's Advisory Committee*, 150.

42. Ibid., 195.

43. Ibid., 196.

44. Ibid., 197.

45. Ibid., 281.

46. Ibid., 291.

47. Ibid., 295.

48. Ibid., 305.

49. Ibid., 312.

50. Ibid., 365.

51. Ibid., 378.

52. *R. v. Agozzino et al.*, 1 C.C.C. 380, 381 (1970). See Appendix A.

53. The term "detrimental reliance" is a shorthand term which originated in the law of contract to describe a situation in which a party relinquishes some property or legal rights based upon the expectation of receiving something in return. The term describes one situation in which courts have found it necessary to enforce a promise in order to achieve justice -- i.e., where the party complaining that the promise was broken had acted in reliance on the promise and had done so to his detriment in the sense that he had already relinquished something of value when the promise was broken.

54. *Frank Richard Turner*, 54 Cr.App.R. 352 (C.C.A. 1970).

55. Ibid.
56. Ibid.
57. Ibid.
58. R. v. Brown, 8 C.C.C. (2d) 227 (O.C.A. 1972). See Appendix A.
59. *Attorney General of Canada v. Roy*, 18 C.R.N.S. 89 (Que.Q.B 1972). See Appendix A.
60. *R. v. Wood*, 26 C.C.C. (2d) 100 (Atla.A.C., App. Div. 1975). See Appendix A.
61. Ibid.
62. *Perkins & Pigeau v. The Queen*, 35 C.R.N.S. 222 (Que.C.A. 1976). See Appendix A.
63. *Regina v. Roy*, 32 C.C.C. (2d) 97 (O.C.A. 1976). See Appendix A.
64. *Her Majesty the Queen v. Daniel Charles Talbot* (unreported case, no. 454/76, of the O.C.A. released Dec. 14, 1976, Houldon, Martin & Blair, J.J.A.). See Appendix A.
65. *Regina v. Arthur*, 39 C.C.C. (2d) 158 (P.E.I.S.C., App.Div. 1978). See Appendix A.
66. *Regina v. Ferrio & Richards* (reported in Crowns Newsletter, April 1979, p. 39, Ont.Co.Ct., April 3, 1979). See Appendix A.
67. Justice Cou, District Court Judge, interview by author, Toronto, Ontario, June 1989.
68. *Regina v. Johnston & Tremayne*, 4 C.C.C. 64 (O.C.A. 1970). See Appendix A.
69. *Regina v. Greene*, 20 C.R.N.S. 238 (Ont.Co.Ct. 1971)
70. "Defending a Criminal Case," *Special Lectures of the Law Society of Upper Canada, 1969: Panel Discussion--Problems in Advocacy and Ethics* (Toronto: Richard De Boo Limited, 1969), 299.
71. *Her Majesty the Queen v. Kirkpatrick*, Que.C.A. 337 (1971). See Appendix A.
72. *Regina v. Pretty*, 5 C.C.C. (2d) 332 (P.E.I.S.C., C.C.A. 1971). See Appendix A.
73. *Regina v. Fleury*, 23 C.R.N.S. 164 (Que.C.A. 1971). See Appendix A.
74. *Regina v. Cusack*, 41 C.C.C. (2d) 289 (N.S.S.C., App.Div. 1978). See Appendix A.
75. *Regina v. Joseph Lapointe*, 2 W.C.B. 199 (1978). See Appendix A.
76. The Law Reform Commission of Ontario, *Report on Administration of Ontario Courts, Part II* (Toronto: Department of Justice, 1973), 119.
77. Ibid.
78. Ibid., 124.
79. Ibid.
80. Ibid.
81. Justice Arthur Martin, Ontario Court of Appeals at the time of the interview, interview by author, Toronto, Ontario, March 11, 1987.
82. Special Lectures of the Law Society of Upper Canada, "Defending a Criminal Case," (1969): 309.

83. Ibid.

84. The Law Reform Commission of Ontario, *Administration of Ontario Courts*, 120.

85. "At a Glance, Plea Bargaining," *Chitty's Law Journal* 24 (1978): 78-79.

86. Ibid.

87. Ibid.

88. *Globe & Mail*, December 13, 1971.

89. The Law Reform Commission of Ontario, *Administration of Ontario Courts*, 122-123.

90. Curt T. Griffiths, John Klein, and Simon N. Verdun-Jones, *Criminal Justice in Canada: An Introductory Text* (Vancouver: Butterworth & Jones, 1980), 161.

91. Michael Innes, Chief Provincial Crown Attorney, interview by author, tape recording, Toronto, Ontario, March 12, 1987.

92. Gerard A. Ferguson and Darrell W. Roberts, "Plea Bargaining: Directions for Canadian Reform," *The Canadian Bar Review* 52 (1974): 497-576.

93. Ed Galler, Provincial Crown Attorney, interview by author, tape recording, Toronto, Ontario, March 12, 1987. Interviewed by the author again, March, 1997.

94. Sarah Welch, Provincial Crown Attorney, interview by author, tape recording, Toronto, Ontario, March 12, 1987; Dambrot, interview. Interviewed by the author again, March, 1997.

95. D. Aford et al., *Some Statistics on the Preliminary Inquiry in Canada* (Toronto: Department of Justice, 1984), 10.

96. Dambrot, interview.

97. Welch, interview.

98. Ibid.

99. Ibid.

100. Ferguson, "Directions for Canadian Reform," 541-54.

101. Special Lectures of the Law Society of Upper Canada, "Defending a Criminal Case," 69-76.

102. Rosenberg, interview.

103. *Corpus Almanac: Canadian Source Book* (Don Mills, Ontario: Corpus Information Services, 1985), 16-17.

104. Martin, interview; Cou, interview.

105. LeSage, interview.

106. *Adgey v. The Queen*, C.C.C. (2d) 1977 (1973).

107. Stenning, *Appearing for the Crown*, 225.

108. *See Rex v. Hand*, 3 D.L.R. 128 (1946). *See also Rex v. Forde*, 17 Cr. App. R. 99 (1932), and *Rev v. Taylor*, 34 Cr. App. R. 138 (1950).

109. Cousineau, *Setting Standards*, 295-96.

110. Griffiths, Klein, and Verdun-Jones, *Criminal Justice in Canada*, 164.

111. *R. v. Simoneau*, 40 C.C.C. (2d) 307 (1978).

112. Ibid.

113. D. W. Perras, "Plea Negotiation," *Saskatchewan Law Review* 44 (1979): 143.

CHAPTER 4
THE ORIGINS OF PLEA BARGAINING IN THE UNITED STATES

Hagan and Leon's characterization of the Americans' system of criminal justice as a due process model is based heavily on the provisions of the Bill of Rights in the United States Constitution, which have been in place since 1791. An examination of the behavior of the judiciary in the United States in the nineteenth and early twentieth centuries in relation to plea bargaining demonstrates the manner in which the due process model was carried out at that time.

The Emergence Of Plea Bargaining

Plea bargaining originated in English common law courts in the 1700's.[1] Early in the development of plea bargaining in England, accomplices in felony cases were "either pardoned . . . upon the defendant's conviction or executed . . . upon the defendant's acquittal."[2] Increasingly, plea bargaining of this nature became discredited as, according to Yvette Beeman, "the likelihood of perjury by the accomplice was thought to outweigh the probative value of his testimony."[3]

According to many criminal justice historians, plea bargaining in the United States was scarce until the mid-nineteenth century. The criminal justice historian, Samuel Walker, notes that while the historical origins of plea bargaining in the United States remains obscure, fragmentary evidence indicates that guilty pleas in the United States had become a major device for disposing of cases by the middle of the 19th Century, and were probably the dominant method by the end of the century.

John H. Langbein, another commentator on the history of plea bargaining has observed that, as late as the eighteenth century, the ordinary jury trial was a judge-dominated, lawyer-free procedure conducted so rapidly that plea bargaining was unnecessary.[4] Juries often heard several cases before retiring, and the law of evidence was underdeveloped. Therefore, the administrative pressure for plea bargaining was small.[5] Most serious crimes were punishable by death, so guilty pleas were considered ill-advised, and trial was thought the safest test of justice.[6]

In the latter part of the nineteenth century the number of criminal trials began to decline. Both in England and in the United States the criminal process was undergoing a transformation from a lay administrative process to one dominated by legally trained full-time professional advocates. During this time period, both pretrial procedures and the rules of evidence expanded in number and complexity.[7]

As the number of trials declined, the jury played a less important role in the criminal process and the prosecutor rose in prominence. Prosecutors were swamped by the rising load of criminal cases. In 1863 in Cuyahoga County, Ohio, the Cleveland prosecutor handled 60 indictments. By 1880, two prosecutors handled 187 indictments, and by 1900, three individuals handled 512 cases. The numbers continued to increase during the next two decades. By 1920 there were six attorneys in the prosecutor's office, but the number of cases had risen to 2,762.[8] Similarly, another observer of plea bargaining found that in Connecticut between 1880 and 1910 only slightly more than 10% of criminal cases went to trial.[9]

One of the leading authorities on the development of plea bargaining indicates that plea bargaining in the United States emerged as a significant practice only after the American Civil War.[10] Early common law treatises, including those dating from the seventeenth century, indicate that courts were reluctant to accept guilty pleas. These treatises declared that a "confession" was not a pleading at all.[11] Elaborate categories of pleas were offered to defendants at criminal trials, but never contained the possibility of confession or guilty pleas.

Later treatises on evidence from the nineteenth century set forth the law of guilty pleas, stipulating that confessions must be voluntary. Confessions could be grouped into one of four categories: extrajudicial confessions, confessions during preliminary interrogation by magistrates, confessions resembling pleas of *nolo contendere*, and confessions that today would be termed guilty pleas. It has been suggested that the lack of differentiation between confessions and guilty pleas lead historians to the conclusion that "courts would have condemned the practice of plea bargaining had they had occasion to do so."[12]

Despite the above observations, early practices which had characteristics of plea bargaining in fact existed in the United States prior to the 1800's. For example, in many jurisdictions, a felon able to flee to a church, was permitted sanctuary at the church, and, if he subsequently confessed his crime, was permitted to "abjure the realm," or in other words, suffer exile and a forfeiture of goods, rather than conviction and judicially imposed punishment.[13] As another example, "compounding" a crime at common law also was frequently practiced. Rather than stand trial, the defendant would offer money in return for the victim's refusal to prosecute. In both cases, the courts and society accepted something short of the justice demanded by the Hebraic code -- an eye for an eye, etc.

Another pre-1800's practice with attributes possibly foreshadowing plea bargaining was the practice of "approvement." An accused felon, before a judge, would confess his crime to the judge and offer to bring a private prosecution against other participants in the same crime. If the judge accepted the offer, the defendant was automatically pardoned. "Approvement" eventually fell out of favor, but judicial discretion was retained to allow a felon to testify against his accomplice. The leniency inherent in the practice of "approvement" was, by its very nature, reserved to the judiciary and bargaining by the prosecutor was strictly forbidden.[14] Later, however, by the 1870's, a number of jurisdictions had allowed the public prosecutor to displace the trial judge in performing this function. Courts favored this development because the prosecutor could, in light of other evidence already obtained, better assess the need for the testimony of an additional accomplice.[15] Nevertheless, being an era when jury trials were still extremely rapid, pleading not guilty was more common and favored in the law.[16] Defendants were encouraged to stand trial, even if they initially had pleaded guilty.

Reasons For The Development Of Plea Bargaining

The rise of professional police and prosecutors also led to a decline of trials and the rise of plea bargaining in the United States.[17] Changing ideas of punishment and sentencing, as well as the expansion of substantive criminal law, perhaps as a result of increased urbanization and industrialization, contributed to the rise of plea bargaining practices.

Plea bargaining in the late nineteenth century mirrored the broader structural developments underlying the criminal justice system as a whole.[18] The development of plea bargaining was most likely related to the broad structural changes developing in the role of the courts. Formerly, courts were able to control their own caseloads. By the late nineteenth century, however, courts lost their dominant position in criminal justice due to the rise of police and prosecutorial staffs which began to handle arrest and charging decisions.[19]

The rise of plea bargaining also may be linked to overcrowded conditions in state and local prisons.[20] Without a place to go upon sentencing, some sort of deal needed to be worked out. A study of plea bargaining in Alameda County, California from 1880-1970 by Lawrence M. Friedman, however, found it difficult to attribute plea bargaining to crowded dockets and heavy caseloads because there is evidence of plea bargaining in the Superior Court of Alameda County from its very beginning in 1880.[21] Friedman downplays studies tracing how and why plea bargaining began as nothing more than guesswork.[22] His criteria for identifying a case as one which was plea bargained is basically, "he knows one when he sees one."[23] Friedman further claims that "plea bargaining cannot be explained simply as a reaction to crowded court conditions. It is connected with structural and social changes in criminal justice, in particular, the rise of professional police and prosecutors."[24] In addition to the Alameda County study, numerous other studies suggest that plea bargaining was commonplace to the time when overcrowding became a factor.

During the early part of the twentieth century, criminal codes were revised and became more complex; new laws of evidence, including the exclusionary rule, were instated,[25] and counsel for both the state and the defendant became more common. The role of the amateur in the criminal process decreased. Pretrial activity increased and, as part-time lawyers declined, full-time persons took their place.[26] Trials became increasingly complicated. And as a result, trials were no longer used as the principal means of dealing with serious crime.

The increase in crime brought about by increased population densities, combined with the more complicated procedures, worked to delay the rapid conclusion of prosecutions. Presumably as a result of the above factors, there was more widespread reliance on plea bargaining.[27]

By the turn of the century the courts came into their peak of power and effectiveness in the operation of government.[28] More than ever, the courts took decision-making power for themselves -- a trend which allowed the courts to assume greater authority over plea bargaining. This power was further influenced by the growing tendency of citizens to take their grievances to court and to rely on the legal system for the resolution of their disputes. This reliance, in turn, created an even greater caseload and need for even more legal professionals.

The strains on the criminal justice system can be seen in the comments of President William H. Taft, in his address before the Civic Forum of New York City on April 28, 1908:

> And now, what has been the result of the lax administration of criminal law in this country? Criminal statistics are exceedingly difficult to obtain. The number of homicides one can note from the daily newspapers, the number of indictments, trials, convictions, acquittals, or mistrials it is hard to find. Since 1885 in the United States there have been 131,951 murders and homicides and there have been 2,286 executions. In 1885, the number of murders was 1,808. In 1904, it has increased to 8,482. The number of executions in 1885 was 108. In 1904, it was 116. This startling increase in the number of murders and homicides as compared with the number of executions tells the story. As murder is on the increase, so are all offenses of the felony class, and there can be no doubt that they will continue to increase unless the criminal laws are enforced with more certainty, more severity, than they now are.[29]

Prior to 1914, the criminal justice system exhibited an extensive use of probation. Shortly thereafter, there was a change in the attitude of the public.[30] The growing middle class demanded a higher level of law and order. Thus, a shift of judicial philosophy to the opposite extreme (from a liberal approach to a law and order approach) appeared in the attitude of the courts. A gradual shutting off of the judicial "parole" further forced the criminal lawyers to look for other sources of relief, such as, plea bargaining.

Disfavor Of The Courts In The 1800's

The case of *Commonwealth v. Battis* (1804)[31] is consistent with the contention that plea bargaining may not have developed until after the Civil War, and that American courts followed the practice of encouraging defendants to go to trial. This case, the first known American decision on the guilty plea, involved a twenty-year-old black man accused of raping and murdering a thirteen-year-old white girl. The defendant pleaded guilty to those charges of rape and murder, provoking the court to inform him that "he was under no legal or moral obligation to plead guilty -- but that he had a right to deny the several charges and put the government on proof of them." Nevertheless, the defendant maintained his guilty plea. He was subsequently sent back to prison to reconsider. Upon his second return to court he again pleaded guilty.

The court ordered an examination of the sanity of this defendant and of whether "there had . . . been tampering with him, either by promises, persuasion, or hopes of pardon if he would plead guilty." No such evidence was discovered, the guilty plea was entered, and the defendant was executed. While this case appears to be accepted as the first known case of plea bargaining, it is unlikely that this decision was essential in the initiation of the practice of plea bargaining.

When the practice of formal plea bargaining began to emerge in the United States around the time of the Civil War, the courts expressed disapproval and reluctance to accept the concept. For example, in *Swang v. State* (1865),[32] the defendant pleaded guilty and was fined thirty-five dollars on two counts of gambling. Eight other charges of gambling were dismissed as a result of an agreement with the prosecutor. The Tennessee Supreme Court ordered a new trial:

> [this] statement of fact [was] unprecedented in the history of the state. . . .[the defendant was] among other things highly improper, told by the Attorney General, that if he did not submit, he would have to go to jail, and that he certainly could prove his guilt. The plea of guilty was entered . . . while the prisoner was protesting against his guilt, but as the best, under the circumstances, he could do.[33]

Courts throughout the country expressed similar sentiments of disfavor against the greater frequency of guilty pleas. In *People v. McCrory* (1871),[34] the California Supreme Court stated:

> A party should not be allowed to trifle with the Court by deliberately entering a plea of "guilty" one day and capriciously withdrawing it the next. But when there is reason to believe that the plea has been entered through inadvertence, and without due deliberation, or ignorantly, and mainly from the hope that the punishment, to which the accused would otherwise be exposed, may thereby be mitigated, the Court should be indulgent in permitting the plea to be withdrawn.[35]

In *Wright v. Rindskopf* (1877),[36] the Supreme Court of Wisconsin expressed its concern about plea bargaining and its secrecy, but further criticized the actions of the public prosecutor.

> An agreement of the public prosecutor, unsanctioned by the court (if such sanction could be given in such a case), for immunity or clemency to several defendants, in several indictments, upon one of them becoming a witness for the prosecution upon still other indictments, would be a fraud upon the court, and an obstruction of justice.[37]

As guilty plea cases came before the courts with increasing frequency in the nineteenth century, the judicial response was expressed in statements such as: "The law favors a trial on the merits."[38] Where plea bargaining was accepted, it was on condition that the plea be entirely voluntary by one competent to know its consequences and should not be introduced because of fear, misapprehension, persuasion, promises, inadvertence or ignorance.

THE EMERGENCE OF A NEW PHILOSOPHY

Building upon the idea of enlightenment in the late nineteenth century, a number of factors had a broad impact on criminal procedures, including the increasing industrialization of the United States, and the idea of rehabilitation as a penological goal. The most striking feature of this period, aside from the reformers' obsession with order and regimentation, was their optimism. They never doubted that most of the criminals could eventually be cured with a carefully controlled environment. Reformers were also confident that penitentiaries, by providing models of discipline, industry, and stability, would have a therapeutic influence on the society at large.[39] As a result, a movement for "new penology" emerged. A criminal act was interpreted simply as one of the many symptoms of a defective or infected personality in need of treatment. It followed that the duration and severity of treatment should not be equated to the crime, but should be contingent on a patient's receptivity to therapy -- that is, to his behavior on probation or within a reformatory institution. This philosophy introduced new procedures which, in the hopes of reforming and rehabilitating the offender, permitted court officials more discretion in sentencing.[40] Thus, in 1870, the National Prison Congress held at Cincinnati for the first time proposed sentences of indeterminate length that would leave "proof of reformation" to the criminal. The prisoner's destiny was placed in his own hands.

Reformers widened and made legitimate the discretionary authority of various officials and administrators.[41] Prosecuting attorneys and judges, ordinarily sensitive to any allegation of "coddling" offenders, discovered that probation and indeterminate sentences made plea bargaining easier and decreased crowded court calendars. When journalists blamed judges for allowing convicts to terrorize society, the judges could shift the blame to parole boards and probation officers, who were less vulnerable to political pressure and who, in general, benefitted from the professional prestige conferred on them by discretionary power. The progressive reforms of the late nineteenth and early twentieth century valued individual initiative and self-respect, deplored rigid codes and procedures that affected individual differences, and imposed categorical limits on individual "development." The hallmark of the progressive programs was the individual "case study" and the demand for "discretionary responses to each case."

This classical period of penology was undoubtedly too optimistic in its views concerning human nature. However, that attitude was a welcomed contrast to the traditional practice of resorting to revenge and harsh criminal procedures, without regard to the interest of truth, society as a whole, or the way in which criminal justice was perceived by society at large.

Surprisingly, the development of plea bargaining attracted little attention. Given the prominent role of the jury, particularly in the early part of the 19th Century, one would expect that its gradual demise would cause some alarm. Enoch Wines and Theodore Dwight were among the few people to note this. In their 1867 survey of prisons, they appended a questionnaire investigating different aspects of criminal process. Two questions dealt with plea bargaining. A respondent from Connecticut indicated that more than one-half of those arraigned pleaded guilty. In Kentucky, the proportion that pleaded guilty was small.[42] Apparently plea bargaining did not arouse concern until later. The increased use of negotiated plea, involving the gradual eclipse of the jury and enlarged role of the prosecutor, was also part of the general trend toward bureaucratic specialization. The public played a decreasing direct role in the administration of criminal justice as particular tasks were assumed by specialized bureaucracies. Viewed in long-range terms, the prosecutor replaced the jury, just as the professional police replaced the citizen nightwatch.[43]

COURTS' CONTINUED DISFAVOR IN THE EARLY 1900'S

The courts in the early 1900'S, however, still showed a reluctance to accept such a plea because doing so could make the system appear to be compromised.

> As the plea of guilty is often made because the defendant supposes that he will thereby receive some favor of the court in the sentence, it is the English practice not to receive such plea unless it is persisted in by the defendant after being informed that such a plea will make no alteration in the punishment . . . [J]udicial discretion . . . should always be exercised in favor of innocence and liberty. All courts should so administer the law as to secure a hearing upon the merits if possible.[44]

In a case in 1908 the Supreme Court of Florida stated:

> A plea of guilty should be entirely voluntary by one competent to know the consequences, and should not be induced by fear, misapprehension, persuasion, promises, inadvertence or ignorance.[45]

Throughout the latter part of the nineteenth century and into the early twentieth century, it seems that the judiciary was on guard against coercion, undue influence, and other behind-the-scenes conduct that might have tainted any plea bargaining. Plea bargaining was scrutinized with suspicion. Judges seemed to prefer the "truth finding" process of an adversarial proceeding in open court before a jury. This outlook is consistent with the idealistic legal philosophies of the time under which the activities of the judiciary were seen as a high-minded pursuit of a pre-existing, naturally occurring body of law, and trials were believed to be, if properly controlled and perfected, a theoretically ideal "engine of truth." By following this approach and shunning plea bargaining, the judiciary of the time may have acted as vigilant gatekeepers against the tyranny of the state over the rights of the individual.

As mentioned previously, this state of affairs began to change by the early twentieth century. By this time, changing legal philosophies coupled with increasing urbanization and other pressures on the system resulted in a rapid transition to plea bargaining in major urban centers. This was not without criticism however. In the 1920's, plea bargaining was criticized as a device for enabling politically connected defendants to gain preferential treatment.[46] But its condemnation continued to center around the coercion involved in "forcing" a defendant to plead guilty. As discussed later, these attitudes changed drastically as the twentieth century progressed.

NOTES

1. Yvette A. Beeman, "Accomplice Testimony Under Contingent Plea Agreements," *Cornell Law Review* 72 (1987): 800. Under the common law system, English laws consisted of a body of opinions written by judges called "case law." Lawrence M. Friedman, *American Law: An Introduction* (New York: W. W. Norton & Company, 1984), 16. The doctrine of "precedent" that requires judges to follow previous case law decisions governs the common law system. Ibid. During the eighteenth and nineteenth centuries, the English rejected the adoption of a civil law system based on a set of codes enacted by a legislative body, and maintained their strong adherence to the common law system. Early English settlers brought the common law tradition to America in the 1700's. The English common law tradition quickly became the core of American law during the 1800's. Morton J. Horwitz, *The Transformation of American Law: 1780-1860* (Cambridge, Mass.: Harvard University Press, 1977), 4. The only American state that adopted the civil law tradition was Louisiana, a state with a strong French heritage.

2. Beeman, "Accomplice Testimony," 800.

3. Ibid., 801.

4. John H. Langbein, "Understanding the Short History of Plea Bargaining," *Law and Society Review* 13 (1979): 261.

5. Ibid., 261.

6. Alschuler, "Plea Bargaining History," 216.

7. Malcolm H. Feeley, "Plea Bargaining and the Structure of the Criminal Process," *Justice System Journal* 7 (Winter 1982): 338.

8. Samuel Walker, *Popular Justice, A History of American Criminal Justice* (New York: Oxford University Press, 1980), 112.

9. *See* Heumann, *Plea Bargaining.*

10. Alschuler, "Plea Bargaining History," 211.

11. Ibid., 218.

12. Ibid., 219.

13. Ibid.

14. Ibid., 219-20.

15. Ibid., 220.

16. Jonathan D. Casper, *American Criminal Justice: The Defendant's Perspective* (Englewood Cliffs, N.J.: Prentice-Hall, 1972), 214-215.

17. Ibid.

18. Mark Haller, "Plea Bargaining, The Nineteenth Century Context," *Law and Society Review* 13 (1979): 273-279.

19. Ibid.

20. Ibid.

21. In 1880, Albert McKenzie was accused of embezzling $52.50 from the Wilcox and Gibbs Sewing Machine Company. He initially pleaded guilty to the offense. At his trial he came forward with his lawyer and asked to withdraw his plea, in favor of pleading guilty to an amount less than $50.00. This bargain was consented to by the District Attorney and allowed by the court which sentenced McKenzie to 6 months in jail. Lawrence M. Friedman, "Plea Bargaining in Historical Perspective," *Law and Society Review* 7 (1979): 249; Lawrence M. Friedman, "The Devil is not Dead: Exploring the History of Criminal Justice," *Georgia Law Review* 11 (1972): 257.

22. Friedman, "Plea Bargaining in Historical Perspective," 247.

23. Ibid.

24. Ibid.

25. Ibid. *See also* Lawrence M. Friedman, *A History of American Law* (New York: W. W. Norton & Company, 1984).

26. Feeley, "Perspectives on Plea Bargaining," 201.

27. Jay Wishingrad, "Plea Bargaining in Historical Perspective," *Buffalo Law Review* 23 (1974): 525.

28. *See* Skolnick, "Social Control."

29. "Criminal Statistics in Anglo-Saxon Countries," *Canadian Law Journal* LIII (1917): 368.

30. Ibid.

31. *Commonwealth v. Battis*, 1 Mass. 95 (1804).

32. *Swang v. State*, 42 Tenn. 212 (1865).

33. Ibid., 212-14.

34. *People v. McCrory*, 41 Cal. 458, 462 (1871).

35. Ibid.

36. *Wright v. Rindskopf*, 43 Wis. 344 (1877).

37. Ibid.

38. Alschuler, "Plea Bargaining History," 224.

39. *See* David J. Rothman, *Conscience and Convenience: The Asylum and its Alternatives in Progressive America* (Boston: Little, Brown, 1980).

40. Lynn M. Mather, "Comments on the History of Plea Bargaining," *Law and Society Review* 13 (1979): 281.

41. *See* Rothman, *Conscience and Convenience.*

42. *See* Walker, *Popular Justice.*

43. Ibid.

44. *Deloach v. State*, 77 Miss. 691 (1900), in Alschuler, "Plea Bargaining History," 224.

45. *Pope v. State*, 56 Fla. 81, 47 So. 487 (1908).

46. Peter F. Nardulli, "Plea Bargaining: An Organizational Perspective," *Journal of Criminal Justice* 6 (Fall 1978): 217-231.

CHAPTER 5

THE EARLY PERIOD OF PLEA BARGAINING IN CANADA

By the middle of the 19th century guilty pleas had become a major device for handling criminal cases in Canada. While the existing literature concerning the historical origins of the practice is limited in the United Sates, in Canada it is virtually nonexistent. According to one Canadian commentator, "there is not a single comprehensive published historical account of any aspect of the criminal justice history in Canada."[1] The history of plea bargaining in Canada is unknown, since there are no historical works that address this issue.[2]

Perhaps this can be attributed to the fact that the history of a reporting system in Canada did not start until 1892, subsequent to the adoption of the Canadian criminal code.[3] It was not until 1892 that the first volume of Canadian criminal cases was published.[4] Justice Arthur Martin, who at one time was the associate editor of the *Canadian Criminal Reporter*, stated that in the early 1900s "very little came out of the criminal courts in the way of judgment in criminal law."[5] Apparently the problem was not one of selecting the noteworthy cases out of a large collection but rather was to find enough material to publish a volume each year.

Nonetheless, there are a small number of Canadian cases in the early twentieth century in which plea bargaining is mentioned. Based on these cases, it is evident that some opposition to plea negotiation existed at the time. These early cases exhibit the historical attitude of the profession toward plea bargaining as a tainted practice, which is similar to the attitudes shared by the American judiciary at the same time.

Significant debate over the values of plea bargaining started much later in Canada then it did in the United States. Nonetheless, it is evident from what little can be found on the subject in the early part of the century, that the Canadian courts treated "guilty" pleas with careful consideration and, in instances where the plea was ambiguous, the courts quashed the conviction. This is illustrated by the few provincial cases before 1920 discussed below.

DISFAVOR OF THE COURTS ON THE GUILTY PLEAS

An examination of available records and literature reveals only three cases prior to the 1920s which even remotely deal with guilty pleas. In the first of these, *R. v. Swett* (1914),[6] the defendant purported to plead guilty to a charge of being a frequenter of a disorderly house in these words: "I was there if that makes me guilty." The lower court failed to appreciate that the admission of being there on one occasion was not equivalent to an admission that he was in the habit of frequenting it. As a result, the Supreme Court of Alberta quashed the conviction.[7]

Similarly, in *R. v. Golathan* (1915),[8] the defendant was charged with entering a dwelling at night with intent to steal. The defendant admitted to having entered the dwelling but not for the purpose of stealing. Again, the Court of Criminal Appeals held that the accused must not be taken to have admitted his guilt unless he does so in unmistakable terms.[9]

In *R. v. Ingleson* (1915),[10] the court's concern was over the ambiguity of the defendant's plea. In this case, the defendant was charged with knowingly receiving stolen horses. The accused pleaded guilty to the charge but, prior to sentencing, handed to the Court of Criminal Appeals a written statement which read: "I am guilty of taking the horses not knowing them to be stolen."[11] The Court of Criminal Appeals held that a plea of not guilty should have been entered and that the matter must be sent back for a new trial. The rationale behind the above court decision was that no person should be seen to give up any right accorded to him unless there is a clear indication that he intends to give up that right.[12]

From these few cases, it appears that Canadian judges exercised a certain level of caution with respect to accepting an admission of guilt. As we will see in later chapters, this level of caution still continues to be exercised.

Since there is no historical analysis of plea negotiations available in the literature, the historical origin and development of this practice remains something of a mystery in the Canadian legal history. There is no evidence that plea bargaining was a dominant method of case disposition at this time or that there was a need or desire to adopt regulations tending to routinize the practice.

Historical Differences Between United States And Canada

The histories of the United States and Canada potentially provide insights which account for differences in plea bargaining practices and attitudes between the two nations. Hagan and Leon's assertion of greater Canadian adherence to crime control perhaps is influenced by the lack of existence (prior to the adoption of the Canadian Charter of Rights and Freedoms in 1982) of something equivalent to the provisions of the United States Bill of Rights as it pertains to criminal procedure.[13]

Moreover, Canada and the United States launched their respective governments under very different conditions. Canada developed through gradual evolution whereas the United States sprang up from a revolution. According to Goldberg and Mercer, Americans place a greater emphasis on the individual as compared to Canadians, who seem to value collective efforts.

> It is probably strange and surprising to many Americans that Canada has remained a part of the British Commonwealth of nations. Perhaps this is because it is not generally understood that the only remaining tie between England and Canada is that of choice on our part. . . . the initial difference between Canada and the U.S. is that Britain never exacted any taxes from us. . . . [it was the] British taxpayer who paid for our protection and British troops who protected us. . . . we are different . . . as a result of our respective histories, our different political institutions and affiliations, our relative populations and the way we have each developed economically.[14]

The fathers of the Canadian Confederation spoke of "peace, order, and good government," not "life, liberty, and the pursuit of happiness." The formal characteristics of the two societies are firmly connected in opposite ways to the American Revolution: the pursuit of the goals set out in the 1776 Declaration of Independence and the conduct of social life in the pattern set by the Constitution versus the rejection of revolution, and its transcendental goals, by English-speaking Canada.[15]

The two governments also were set up with different structures -- the parliamentary system versus a congressional system. American government was established on a careful system of checks and balances among the legislature (the Congress), the executive (the President and all of the departments of government that carry out legislated mandates), and the judiciary. Rising above all is the United States Constitution, the sole source of the balance point. In contrast, in the Canadian parliamentary system, the parliament is supreme and its laws constitute "the supreme law of the land." Parliament in Canada has much more power under this system than do Congress and the state legislatures in the United States.[16]

Lipset has traced the national differences between the United States and Canada to the impact of the American Revolution.[17] "In trying in the early fifties to answer the questions what is 'distinctively Canadian,' Frye noted in 'Letters in Canada' that 'historically, a Canadian is an American who rejects the revolution'."[18]

Other scholars have made similar observations from a comparative and historical perspective. Russell Brown concluded his analysis by saying, "the American desire to free oneself from the father [England] is also a desire to escape the past with its tradition and authority."[19]

In one particularly noteworthy summation, Lipset refers an essay by David Potter:[20]

> The United States had a revolution which gave ascendancy to democrats and impaired the prestige of the elite; Canada received a migration of loyalists, many of whom clung to the concept of an elite on the British model as a means of preserving social order . . .
>
> Canadians believed that the state, through some authority, should provide moral direction for the society it governed. Moral direction meant discipline, order, responsibility, obedience, even inhibition. America, too, has believed in discipline, order, responsibility, and the rest, but it has believed in them as self-imposed, through the acceptance of a Protestant ethic, not imposed by public authority . . . . Therefore, Americans have countenanced not only extremes of freedom and permissiveness, but even violence, corruption, license and social deviancy in preference to a public authority strong enough to control them. Perhaps there can be no more basic difference in social philosophy than the one illustrated by these diverse attitudes.[21]

Lipset also writes of Ronald Sutherland's book, *The New Hero*, where Sutherland, a student of Canadian Literature, summed up his observations concerning the Canadian and American differences:

> American puritanism, developing as it did from the peculiar notions of a small and persecuted sect, underlined self-reliance and the responsibility of the individual . . . . Canada, by contrast, had relatively sophisticated church systems among both Catholics and Protestants. New England puritanism and subsequent evangelical movements called for personal seeking of God. Working out one's salvation in 'fear and trembling.' Canadians, on the other hand, had the security of reliance upon a church establishment, detailed codes of behavior, a controlling system and; in general, until very recently, Canadians have tended to depend upon and to trust systems which control their lives.[22]

Lipset refers to the work of Samual D. Clark, a Canadian sociologist, in *Angus Volume* where Clark summarized his findings on Canadian and American differences in the following terms:

> . . . we . . . come across the idea that Canadian . . . life is simpler, more honest, more moral than life in the United States, that it lies closer to the rural virtues and has achieved urbanization without giving the same scope to corrupting influence which has been afforded them in the United States.[23]

In the past, the Canadian procedural law in the criminal process area had not been reinforced by written constitutional proscriptions and prohibitions as procedural law had been in the United States. But the Canadian criminal procedure in the past had been fashioned on the whole on a degree of substantial justice in the absence of expressly entrenched rights.

The available evidence, or lack thereof, shows no indication of concerns about plea bargaining before the mid-1900s in Canada. The three cases discussed above show that the only issue related to the entry of guilty pleas was the question of whether the actions of the accused fit the definition of the crime. This state of the historical record may be taken as an indication that plea bargaining was not taking place to any appreciable degree in Canada before the mid-1900s. This would be consistent with the noted differences in the historical roots and cultures of the U.S. and Canada in that a more orderly, less individualistic society would put less strain on the criminal justice system and create less incentive for plea bargaining. History has led Canadians to be more conservative in many respects and perhaps more vigilant in their pursuit of law and order even if it sometimes means compromising individual freedoms. This too means less impetus for plea bargaining. In addition, the differences in the philosophical origins of the nations could well have resulted in a greater tendency among the Canadian bar and judiciary to adhere to the formal processes of the system and shun informal shortcuts such as plea bargaining. In contrast, officials and institutions in the United States, themselves the progeny of a revolution, could be expected to be less concerned with the sanctity of the criminal justice system. In any event, it was not until many years later that the historical record shows plea bargaining to have become more common in Canada and was conducted quite differently than in the United States.

NOTES

1. J.G. Woods, "Criminal Justice History in Canada: A Brief Survey of Work in Progress," *Criminal Justice History and International Annual*, (Westport, Conn.: Meckler Publishing, 1984), 123.
2. Author's examination of the existing records at the Ontario Archives, Attorney General's Record, Oral History Collection, and the examination of the existing secondary sources cited in this study.
3. Proclaimed in force July 1, 1893.
4. Justice Arthur G. Martin, Ontario Court of Appeals, interview by Mrs. C.J.N. Kates, November 8, 1983, Oral History Collection, Osgoode Society of Upper Canada, Toronto, Ontario.
5. Ibid.
6. *R. v. Swett*, 7 W.W.R. 608 (1914).
7. Ibid.
8. *R. v. Golathan*, 11 Cr. App. R. 79 (1915).
9. Ibid.
10. *R. v. Ingleson*, 1 K.B. 512 (1915).
11. Ibid.
12. Ibid.
13. "Symposium," *Canadian Bar Review* 37 (1959): 1-21.
14. Paul P. Hutchison, "Canadians and Americans: How They are Different From One Another," *American Bar Association Journal* 42 (Nov. 1956): 1023-1024.
15. *See* Lipset, *Continental Divide*.
16. *See* Michael A. Goldberg and John Mercer, *The Myth of the North American City: Continentalism Challenged* (Vancouver: University of British Columbia Press, 1986).
17. Lipset, "The Cultural Dimension," 151; *See also* Lipset, *Continental Divide*.
18. Lipset, "The Cultural Dimension," 159.
19. Ibid., 119.

20. Sydney F. Wise, *Canada Views the United States: Nineteenth Century Political Attitudes* (Seattle: University of Washington Press, 1967).

21. Lipset, "The Cultural Dimension."

22. Ibid., 124.

23. Ibid., 115.

CHAPTER 6
PLEA BARGAINING IN THE UNITED STATES AFTER 1920

FLAWS OF THE JUSTICE SYSTEM EMERGE

Plea bargaining had become more widespread in the United States by the early part of this century. Simultaneously, in the 1920s, the American criminal justice system, in many cities, was rife with manipulation and abuse due to the local machinery of justice which had developed, sometimes extending to include the judiciary, and sometimes with ties to organized crime. A number of forces and events, which will be discussed in the later portion of this chapter, caused much of the legal profession to question plea bargaining as a method of case disposition.[1]

As a result of unsatisfactory conditions in most areas of the criminal justice system, a number of states and cities conducted criminal justice surveys. These surveys, which offered a far more complete picture of the workings of American criminal courts than was previously available or has since been available, revealed, among other things, a significant dependence on negotiated pleas as methods for case disposition.

The dominance of the guilty plea apparently came as a surprise to some lawyers and judges, since the judges knew that acceptance of such a plea could compromise the system. However, the system called for expeditious disposal of cases.

In 1937 Judge Lummus[2] remarked that the courts were actually trying only one of every five cases, with guilty pleas being accepted from the other four defendants. He elaborated:

> [T]he prosecutor must subordinate almost everything to the paramount need of disposing of his list [of cases] during the sitting [of the court]. Rather than dismiss the excess by nolle *prosequi,*[3] with no penalty, he must induce defendants in fact guilty to plead guilty, in order that some penalty may be imposed. Half a loaf is better than no bread . . . .
>
> If all the defendants should combine to refuse to plead guilty, and should dare to hold out, they could break down the administration of criminal justice in any state in the union. But they dare not hold out, for such as were tried and convicted could hope for no leniency.[4]

In the 1920s, several authors suggested that an increase in plea negotiations (or the "compromise of criminal cases") was associated with the growth of probation and a belief in individualizing the treatment of offenders. Tension existed between the substantive goal of individual rehabilitation and a court procedure which called for sentencing issues to be discussed only after determination of legal guilt.

In 1928, Raymond Moley, who was the director of the Cleveland Survey of Criminal Justice, reported on his survey of dispositional practices of American criminal courts. In the 1920s in New York City guilty pleas accounted for 88% of all convictions; in Cleveland, 86%; in Chicago, 85%; in Des Moines, 79%; and in Dallas, 70%. Moley presented additional figures to show that these higher rates of guilty pleas were not restricted to large or rapidly growing urban centers, but were found in less populated areas with less crowded courts as well.[5] For instance, guilty pleas accounted for 91% of all convictions in rural upstate New York in the 1920s.[6]

The increasing use of plea bargaining led to a variety of abuses. Policemen abused the role they played in the process and, according to an early twentieth century edition of *Wharton's Criminal Evidence*, were known to convince defendants to plead guilty with false promises when, in fact, they were only interested in the extra money they would receive for mileage and transportation of the convict to prison.[7] Justin Miller, writing in the first issue of the *South California Law Review* in 1927, voiced the concern of many when he said:

> There can be no doubt that our system of criminal law administration is dangerous, both to the rights of individuals and to orderly, stable government . . . [t]he poor, friendless, helpless man is most apt to become the one who helps swell the record of conviction. The necessity

> for making a good record . . . may well result in prosecutions overlooking the rights, privileges and immunities of the poor, ignorant felon who . . . is induced to confess crime and plead guilty through hope of reward or fear of extreme punishment.[8]

Political corruption was an ongoing concern in the administration of criminal justice. Court officials, in order to make the particular courtroom to which they were assigned have a good showing in terms of cases handled, tried to convince as many defendants as possible to plead guilty.

An excellent case study illustrating the problems in the criminal justice system at that time was conducted by the Cleveland Foundation in 1921. The Cleveland Foundation analyzed the industrial and population hub of Cleveland, Ohio, which at that time was second only to New York in numbers of headquarters for large public corporations.[9]

The Cleveland Foundation Survey

The Cleveland Foundation, a non-profit civic organization founded in 1914, announced on January 4, 1921, that part of its functions would be:

> 1) to exercise constant surveillance upon the processes of justice, to the end that the public may be constantly informed as to conditions, both good and bad, which exist in the field of criminal justice; and 2) to assist those in authority to make improvements where desirable in the organization and the operation of the agencies of criminal justice.[10]

In the 1920s, there was much concern among the members of the bar about the corruption of the court system but the general public was not aware of these conditions.[11] The first impetus for this survey came from the city welfare agencies which lacked sufficient funds and equipment to prepare the survey themselves. In December of 1919, the secretary of the Welfare Federation's Committee on Delinquency, Professor Chase E. Gehlke of Western Reserve University's Department of Sociology, proposed to the Cleveland Foundation a survey of the problem of adult and juvenile delinquency. From this plan emerged the first comprehensive criminal justice survey ever undertaken in the United States.[12] Under the directorship of Raymond Moley, the Cleveland Foundation, with civic support, launched its efforts to conduct the comprehensive survey in Cleveland. In 1921 the dean of the Harvard Law School, Rosco Pound, whose philosophy at the time was considered "very progressive," and one of his faculty members at that time, Felix Frankfurter, came to Cleveland to complete the final plans for the survey. The survey took place during what was regarded as a "crime wave" in Cleveland and its purpose was to bring the results of the scientific investigations carried by the survey members to the attention of the general public. It was anticipated that the results of the survey would become an effective instrument of social progress.

The result was entitled *The Cleveland Foundation Survey of Criminal Justice in Cleveland, Part I: The Criminal Courts*, headed by Reginald Heber Smith (hereinafter "the *Survey I*") and *Part II: Prosecution*, headed by Hebert B. Ehrmann (formerly Special Assistant to the U.S. Attorney General) (hereinafter "the *Survey II*") (collectively referred to as "the *Survey*"). The *Survey I* stated that:

> Cleveland . . . suffers from an antiquated and cumbersome criminal procedure utterly unsuited to the modern conditions of her industrial urban life. In the fable, the fox was caught, but in Cleveland, if he were a professional fox, he would be very likely to escape.[13]

The authors of the *Survey* further noted that if the local machinery of justice had not already broken down, there was grave danger that further tolerance of then-existing conditions would result in a complete failure of the system.[14]

To the *Survey* authors, any procedure which hinted of a "deal" among lawyers and judges was distrusted. They found that cases were disposed of with "startling rapidity, which rendered it impossible to give attention to those which merited a real examination."[15] According to the authors, Cleveland judges were often prone to follow the clamor of the press and public. When public sentiment was against the accused, "both the good and the wicked travel the same road."[16] The *Survey I* reported:

> When Tom L. Johnson was mayor, a generous humanitarianism not adequately guided by science in the handling of offenders began which did not reach its sentimental climax until the early '20s. The Chief of Police started to release without trial all first offenders in certain minor crimes, became thereby nationally known as "Golden Rule" Kohler. The idea spread from police to judge, from misdemeanor to felony, until an editor of one of the Cleveland papers put it, "a lawyer regarded it as a personal insult if a judge sent his client away." Under the Davis regime this false idealism was perverted into good-fellowism, and the damage was done. Cleveland became an "easy town."[17]

The court system in existence in Cleveland in 1920 consisted of two courts and two prosecutors' offices (municipal court and common pleas court) and a grand jury. The criminal division of the municipal court had jurisdiction over misdemeanors, violations of city ordinances, and preliminary investigations in felony cases. Its decisions were reviewable either by the court of appeals or the common pleas court for errors of law.[18]

A criminal prosecution began when a policeman or prosecuting witness or victim came to the prosecutor's office. If the facts showed that a crime was committed, the prosecutor "issued an affidavit" by merely completing the appropriate form for the particular offense involved with the name of the person charged and the date.[19]

A subsequent "sifting out" process occurred after a summons was issued to the prospective defendant.[20] This summons was issued by a uniformed policeman who served the function of bringing the accused to the prosecutor's office at a time also convenient for the prosecuting witness or victim. In this informal meeting, the prosecutor would examine each party in an attempt to "sift out" the charges. It was estimated in the *Survey I* that more cases were disposed of at this stage without prosecution than were placed on the court docket.[21]

In felony cases, the municipal court thereafter held a preliminary investigation and, upon a finding of probable cause, would bind the defendant over to the grand jury. The grand jury heard the evidence presented by the prosecuting attorney and, if the grand jury agreed with one or more of the charges against the accused, the grand jury would return a "true bill" identifying the crime for which the defendant was indicted. The case then proceeded before a judge of the common pleas court through the usual stages.[22]

The preceding description, however, apparently was quite different from actual practice. Eyewitness testimony paints a bleak portrait of the environment in which the municipal prosecutor performed his function. Alfred Bettman, a writer of *Survey II*, observed:

> I spent the whole morning in this courtroom, arriving promptly at 9. There was as yet no evidence that any court would be held that day, except the docket book lying open on the table and a few stragglers in the spectators' benches. It was fully 9:30 before the judge appeared and fully 9:45 before he got under way. By that time all the seats and aisles were filled with people -- policemen, defendants, lawyers, spectators. The atmosphere of the room was extremely sordid. It was a room about 40 feet square, walls painted in an ugly yellow, made still more ugly by

> accumulated soot, and no decorations of any kind whatever. Though I sat within 15 feet of the bench and witness-chair and strained my ears, I could seldom catch a word of what was going on. From the beginning to end the whole proceeding seemed to me one calculated to impress the spectator with at least the suspicion that the main influence at work was not the evidence or judicial procedure as we know it, but either strange influences not audible in the courtroom or things that were whispered into the ear of the judge.[23]

Further commenting on *Survey II*, Bettman writes:

> Non-appearances seemed to be in fashion at this court. In at least a dozen cases neither the accused nor the policemen nor detectives were present at first. The cases were called again and again, some of them being heard with part of the witnesses present, others apparently going by default. I did not hear the judge order a single person brought in or mention 'contempt' once. He may have done so, but if he did, it was in a whisper.[24]

A "capable" Cleveland attorney, in observation of a particular prosecutor, reported in the *Survey II*:

> Prosecutor Russick then sat down at the trial table and proceeded to read a book, when Case No. 57 was called. This was a case in which Joseph Sklarski was arrested at the insistence of his landlady, with whom he had boarded for one year, on the charge of assault. Neither the prosecuting witness nor the defendant spoke English, and the defendant was asked by an interpreter if he plead guilty or not guilty, without having the charge translated for his benefit. The interpreter then addressed the court as follows: 'Judge, he says that he pleads guilty but he wants a continuance to get a lawyer.' The court then made some inaudible remark, and in a louder voice told the interpreter to put the prosecuting witness on the stand. She then gave her testimony and the defendant was called to the stand. He testified, and without further testimony the court sentenced him to six months and $200 fine and costs, and he was hurried out of the courtroom in spite of the fact that he protested that he wanted a chance to get an attorney. Throughout the proceeding in this case the prosecutor sat at the trial table reading.[25]

These accounts depict the role, or perhaps lack thereof, that the prosecutor played in the trial and disposition of cases. In the midst of this confusion, seventy-one cases were disposed of in less than three hours on the morning of April 22, 1920 in Room 1, which amounted to about two minutes per case.[26] Such figures of an average day indicate that a trial by jury clearly was the exception rather than the rule.

The Cleveland Crime Survey and its authors took the position that the lack of communication and failure to preserve relevant information necessary to the prosecution of accused individuals resulted in too many cases being discharged. As evidence of this, the *Survey* showed that of 1,832 cases, 13% were discharged outright. (See Appendix F, Table I.) Another 10% of the cases were not prosecuted due to the defendant's case being "nolled" or the defendant's lack of "papers." (See Appendix F, Table I.) A "nolle" was announced just as the case was called and it literally represented a conscious decision (for reasons seldom stated) by the prosecutor, not to prosecute.[27] No "papers" meant that the prosecutor had decided early on that the facts did not warrant prosecution and thus did not issue an affidavit. When a case with no papers was called, it resulted in an automatic dismissal.

Other records in the *Survey II* show wide ranging sentence reductions. (See Appendix G, Table II.) The sentence reductions recorded there, often allowed by the same judge in later stages of the same proceedings, presumably resulted from plea bargaining. Many serious charges were reduced to crimes carrying a lesser sentence or a fine and many pleas were changed from innocent to guilty. Some manner of persuasion apparently took place.

Circumstantial evidence of questionable deal making is furnished by the case of Charles McCormack as reported in the *Survey I*. McCormack was arrested on the Public Square of Cleveland on Saturday, April 23, 1921 for pocketpicking on April 21. That same night at about midnight, Assistant Municipal Prosecutor Kriesberg came to Lieutenant C's desk at the police station inquiring about the possibility of a bond for McCormack.

The police blotter contained the words "pocketpicking" and "picked the pocket of William Smith." In a different ink and different handwriting, lines were drawn through these words and the words "petit larceny" and "stolen" were substituted. Petit larceny was a misdemeanor while pocketpicking was a felony. When the case was called before Judge A on Monday morning, McCormack pleaded guilty to the lesser charge and was fined $50 and sentenced to thirty days.

The Cleveland Crime Survey also observed that Section 4583 of the General Code of Ohio at the time expressly permitted the municipal court in a felony case, when the court was of the opinion that the offense charged was only a misdemeanor, to accept a plea of guilty on the misdemeanor and dismiss the felony charge.[28] No requirements or procedures were set forth by the statute, but its very existence indicates the acceptance of the system to practices like plea bargaining.

The authors of the *Crime Commission Survey* were concerned that cases were compromised due to political affiliations and that corruption prevailed in the criminal court system. Such a conclusion is plausible, though plea bargaining itself as a practice was never mentioned in the survey. However, the population growth and an extreme rise in number of arrests and subsequent caseload suggest that plea bargaining must have flourished as a necessary, though potentially corrupt component of expediency in the criminal courts.

The statistics reported in *The Survey* support the conclusion that a variety of factors may have contributed to a rise in informal expedients including plea bargaining. Included among those is data which evidences the incredible population increases and arrest rate increases preceding 1920, as well as the relatively low number of prosecutors employed to handle the workload. (See Appendix H, Table III.)

The Cleveland Crime Survey also attributed the way in which judges were elected to the bench as another factor contributing to abuses in the disposition of cases in Cleveland. In fact, the survey recommended that judges should be appointed rather than elected.[29] The *Survey* stated that a judge facing reelection had to insure his survival by catering to party bosses who controlled the votes, by patronizing certain influential groups -- racial, religious or industrial -- and by generating favorable publicity in the newspapers and otherwise. According to the *Survey*, the labor organizations actively participated in the election of judges, and did not concern themselves with a judge's fairness or ability. "The unions have lost faith in the courts," stated one of their most respected leaders, "they believe the man who has the influence gets by."[30]

To a judge seeking reelection to the bench in Cuyahoga County, the press was crucial. As a result, judges based their sentences on public sentiment about the case.

The surveys of the 1920s in Cleveland concluded that criminals were given more lenient sentences than they deserved. Assuming the character of the cases did not change significantly during this period and prosecutors did not significantly alter their screening practices, it seems probable that most of the increased numbers of guilty plea defendants would have been convicted had they stood trial, with only a minority being acquitted.[31]

Increased plea bargaining might have led some defendants to plead guilty despite the fact that they would not have been convicted at trial. As the percentage of guilty plea convictions grew in the period just preceding the 1920s, both the percentage of convictions at trial and the percentage of acquittals showed a sharp decline.

The *Survey* observed that plea bargains were not in the cause of justice when the judge accepting the plea had not been informed of the full history and circumstances of the accused who was making the plea. As an example, in December 1920 the prosecutor's office in Cleveland wrote:

> These two boys broke into a confectionery store and helped themselves to about $112 worth of cigars and smoking materials. The court accepted a plea of guilty to petit larceny in the case, hence they were sentenced to the workhouse. There is no previous record against these boys.

The "two boys" mentioned were actually two aliases of the same criminal who had an amazingly long police record. Even the previous record of the prisoner, sent by the Bureau of Criminal Identification to the prosecutor's office, containing only such bald facts as arrests and convictions, rarely reached the judge and, in the 1920s, may not even have been known to the particular prosecutor in charge of the case.[32]

THE CLEVELAND ASSOCIATION FOR CRIMINAL JUSTICE

The Bar Association, after the *Survey* reports had been given to the public, selected the *Survey*'s authoring committees in 1921 "to take up with the Cleveland Foundation . . . in establishing an organization for the promotion of efficient administration of justice."[33] This association represented the eyes and ears of the public in the courts of the city and county. From its inception, the Association adopted a single slogan, i.e., "arm the public with facts." Among the many tasks the association performed was to station a court observer in the Felony Room in the Municipal Court of Cleveland, checking the procedure and prosecutions in the felony cases. During 1926 and 1927, a detailed investigation was made of each and every felony charge dismissed in that Court. After the investigation, the Association issued a public statement as follows:

> The weakest link in the administration of criminal justice in this community is found in the Municipal Court of Cleveland where

preliminary examinations are held in felony cases. The Felony Room is crowded and noisy and the hearings lack dignity and efficiency. The Felony Room well merits its nickname, "The Whispering Court of Cleveland."[34]

PRELIMINARY HEARINGS IN MUNICIPAL COURT

Preliminary hearings in felony cases were, at that time, with the consent of the city law director's office, being conducted by the county prosecutor's office. The Association had noted charge after charge dismissed by the Court or reduced to a misdemeanor on the recommendation of the assistant county prosecutor assigned to the room. The Association's investigation revealed that in 1925, 729 cases were resolved in dismissals in comparison to 1930 where only 85 cases were resolved in dismissals. Apparently some improvements took place in those years.

In July 1928 the Association issued a special bulletin entitled "Theoretical Prosecutions" which reads in part as follows:

> Waivers of felony charges and pleas of guilty to lesser offenses for which the penalty inflicted was trivial in comparison with the seriousness of the offense committed, have been a daily occurrence in the Felony Room at Municipal Court. *Statistically* waiver after waiver had added scores of so-called 'successful prosecutions' to the State's credit, apparently producing a great improvement in prosecutions, but actually reflecting little credit on the efficiency of the prosecuting machinery.[35]

For some weeks thereafter, an improvement was apparent.

Nevertheless, not long thereafter, one of the most conspicuous examples of prosecuting dereliction noted by the Association during its existence, occurred in the case of *State of Ohio v. "Mike the Pipe" Shinkman*. Saturday noon, August 9, 1928, Phillip ("Funny Face") Corry was shot and killed in typical gangster fashion in a cigar store at East 55th Street and Woodland Avenue. His assailant drove away in a waiting vehicle. Several weeks later, "Mike the Pipe" Shinkman surrendered at Central Police Headquarters, in company with his attorney, a well-known local politician, and was formally charged with the murder of Corry.

When the case was first called in the Municipal Court, a continuance was granted. When the case was next called, despite the importance of the case and the publicity given it in the local newspapers, a young and apparently uninformed assistant county prosecutor appeared in the courtroom. The Assistant County Prosecutor hesitatingly conducted a stumbling examination of witnesses, which resulted, according to the Association, in little being proven, save the inadequacy and incompetency of the prosecution. The charge against Shinkman was reduced to Manslaughter, bail set at $3000.00, and a week's time granted the State in which to produce additional evidence. The Association was advised by Municipal Court Judge David Moylan that unless the State succeeded in producing *some* evidence when the case was next called, he would be forced to dismiss the charge against Shinkman and set him free.

The Association investigated the case, called a special meeting of its Executive Committee, and two days before the date of the next hearing in the Shinkman case, wrote the County Prosecutor of Cuyahoga County the following letter:

Mr. Edward C. Stanton, Cleveland, County Prosecutor, August 30, 1928.
Cleveland, Ohio.

My Dear Sir:

The case of Mike Shinkman, alias "Mike the Pipe" requires your immediate attention. The next hearing is scheduled for Saturday, September 1st, in the Municipal Court of Cleveland.

The county Prosecutor's Office of Cuyahoga County must not again be reduced to a state of public incoherency by the appearance in court of Mike Shinkman represented by two lawyers of known political influence.

You ought to prosecute this case personally or send James Connell, your Chief Assistant, to represent you. The public has a right to expect this of you.

Respectfully submitted,
THE CLEVELAND ASSOCIATION
FOR CRIMINAL JUSTICE
Dan B. Cull,
President[36]

When the Shinkman case was called in court the following Saturday, County Prosecutor E. C. Stanton himself appeared in court with his first assistant, James C. Connell. Fully a score of other assistant county prosecutors and judges were present. The examination of witnesses and the presentation of evidence was conducted in such a manner that the entry reducing the charge to Manslaughter was vacated, the First Degree Murder charge reinstated, and Shinkman bound over to the Grand Jury without bail. Following his indictment for Murder by the Grand Jury, Shinkman was convicted by a jury in the Court of Common Pleas in less than two hours' time.

THE REORGANIZING OF THE MUNICIPAL COURT BOND SYSTEM

In this same era a practice prevailed in the Municipal Court of Cleveland permitting the Clerk's office to telephone Municipal Court Judges during the nighttime to ascertain the amount of bail required to secure the release from custody of defendants arrested at night, even on felony charges. The judge, of course, neither saw the defendant nor the arresting officer and knew little or nothing of the defendant's criminal record and even less of the evidence in the case.

As an example, the Association reported that on June 23, 1930, a man by the name of William Schiller was arrested and charged with Robbery. Municipal Judges Thomas E. Greene was telephoned at night by the Clerk's office and after a short telephone conversation, set bail at $2500.00. Nonetheless, Chief of Detectives Cornelius W. Cody ordered Schiller held for "Investigation." The following exchange later occurred with Mr. Schiller's attorney, Mr. Kohen:

Kohen: "Your Honor, you set the bail in this case yourself."

Judge: "Yes -- oh -- yes."

Kohen: "I would like to ask your Honor why when you set bail, the police can refuse to release a man?"[37]

The Association reported that Judge Greene neither asked nor waited for an explanation from the police officers present. Reports indicated that his face reddened angrily:

> When I set bail in a case, the police must release 'em," he declared. Then, turning to Chief of Detectives Cody who was standing near the bench: "If they don't release 'em when I set bail, they are in contempt of court. It's a court order. The police must obey it. You police (glaring at Cody) had better get that through some of your thick skulls etc., etc.[38]

The following day the Association's Executive Committee took the court proceedings under advisement, and, fully appreciating the crime condition existing in Cleveland as well as the fact that occurrences of this character, whether intended to or not, encouraged the lawless elements of the city, passed the following resolution:

> WHEREAS, The Cleveland Association for Criminal Justice believes that the amount of bail set by Judge Thomas F. Greene in the Schiller case Tuesday night after a telephone conversation with the Clerk's office, and without consultation with The Cleveland Police Department, was too low:
>
> NOW, THEREFORE, BE IT RESOLVED that it is the sense of the Executive Committee of the Association that the Municipal Court of Cleveland be requested to adopt a rule of court requiring a judicial inquiry into all disputed major felony cases before setting bail, and that both The Cleveland Police Department and the County Prosecutor's Office be represented at such hearing, and
>
> BE IT FURTHER RESOLVED, that it is the sense of the Association that the proceedings which took place in Judge Thomas E. Greene's courtroom were unwarranted and undignified, and the conduct of the judge on the bench as well as his choice of words in referring to members of The Cleveland Police Department in the court-room at which time and in which place he was not on terms of equality with them were unbecoming and regrettable.[39]

A copy of the Association's resolution was sent to Chief Justice John P. Dempsey of the Municipal Court. Within a week's time the practice of setting bail over the telephone was discontinued by order of the Chief Justice.

The above incident involving "Mike the Pipe" as well as the episode involving the bond system are illustrative of the laxity in the Municipal Court observed by the Association. Even in cases involving crimes as heinous as murder, the responsible officials took matters seriously only after prompting by the Association. Such sloppy ad hoc treatment of cases, according to the Association, was pervasive.

THE CRIMINAL JUSTICE SYSTEM ELSEWHERE

In the 1920s political corruption was a serious concern with the criminal justice system in general and with plea bargaining in particular. Illinois was no exception. The Illinois State Attorney's Office was described as "having been looked upon as a means of building up a political machine and of obtaining political power rather than as a prosecuting agency." Professor Andrew A. Bruce who, in 1929, was an investigator for the Illinois Crime Survey, decried the lack of professionalism and stated that "there can be little question that many of the cases reversed by the Supreme Court were reversed on account of errors which the state's attorney and his assistants should never have committed . . . ."[40]

Further, comments were made concerning the extensive use of plea bargaining between the defendants and the state attorney's office which led to a significant loss of faith on the part of the public in the law enforcement body. The frequent reduction of charges from felonies to petty offenses was revealed by the Illinois survey. The report further stated that the state attorney's office was political in nature and that "the judge cannot always close his ears to the request of political leaders for leniency for political defendants, even though he wants to do the right thing."[41] As these abuses came to the attention of the public, debates arose on the value of plea bargaining.

While the president of the Chicago Crime Commission called plea negotiations "paltering with crime" and wanted to remove from office those judges who had permitted felony charges to be reduced to misdemeanors, W.F. Dodd of the Chicago Bar, in his article entitled, "Progress of Preventive Justice" (1920), actually encouraged those who engaged in this practice. He stated, "In the large cities the difficulty in operating the judicial machinery has become greater, the courts are not able to accommodate all those who apply. . . . Something has to be done to obtain more efficient settlement of cases. This is more true of New York, Cleveland, Chicago . . . where courts for small cases have been set up with rules of procedure based upon the plan of having the parties themselves come to an amicable agreement."[42] Of course part of Dodd's statement referred to possible settlement in civil cases, but he also makes similar comments with respect to criminal cases.

It is surprising that Dodd would make such a public statement, knowing that the Chicago Crime Commission statistics showed 110 murders to each 1 million of population in Chicago, as against 9 to the million in Great Britain and 13 to the million in Canada. "This meant that during the year

1919, there were more murders in Chicago with a population of 4 million than in the British Isles with a population of 40 million."[43]

Edwin W. Sims of the Chicago Bar, in an address before the Section of Criminal Law of the American Bar Association in 1921, stated that for many years in Great Britain and Canada murder cases had been generally disposed in sixty or ninety days. This meant that there had been a trial, an appeal, and the execution of the penalty within that time. In American cities, however, there were practically no murder cases being tried within ninety days.[44]

In 1927, Justin Miller, chairman of the Section on Criminal Law and Criminology of the American Bar Association, in his article entitled, "The Compromise of Criminal Cases," stated:

> In theory there should be no compromises of criminal cases. . . . However, recent surveys [referring to the surveys that were conducted around the country concerning the function of the criminal justice system and the courts] have revealed that the greatest case mortality [the extent to which adjustments, settlements and dispositions are made by court officials] in the administration of criminal justice results not from the operation of those rules, but from the various methods of compromise generally in vogue.[45]

The *Chicago Tribune* (April 27, 1928) called the plea bargaining practice an "incompetent, inefficient and lazy method of administering justice." The Illinois Crime Survey argued that criminals believed that the criminal justice system did not mean business and, as a result, were encouraged in their criminal activities.[46]

Arthur Train, an assistant district attorney in Manhattan in the 1930s, wrote that cases existed in which the "entire population of a prison pen" had pleaded guilty, one after another, after persuasion by the court officials.[47] Judge Arthur L. Alarcon felt that, while prosecutors claimed that bargaining was the only way to reduce the backlog, in reality it was simply a way to reduce their work.[48] Others reported that New York City defense attorneys dickered away sentences for money outside the night court during this same era.

As noted, plea bargaining had a long history that predated the reported dramatic increases in crime and arrests of the prior decades. By 1934, two-thirds of all guilty pleas began with prior pleas of not guilty. Among those who switched, almost half involved pleas to a lesser or fewer charges than they had originally faced. The only striking difference in the disposition pattern since the 1930s had been the increased tendency to plead guilty to a lesser charge or fewer charges, a practice that clearly indicates plea bargaining, and more recent contentions that the adversary process is being replaced by a cooperative bureaucratic process that relies upon the guilty plea.[49] As Frank Remington states, "[t]he crime surveys of the 1920s and 1930s documented for the first time the enormous dependence of the American justice system on plea bargaining."[50]

RELATED JUDICIAL PRONOUNCEMENTS

Following World War II, the criminal justice system in the United States was subjected to further study and reevaluation. Wary of the growing power of the Communist Bloc of nations, increased emphasis was placed on internal security measures and on regulation of business practice and strengthening of national defense. During 1950-1951, the Kefauver Committee Hearings on Interstate Crime were carried on national television and resulted in sweeping removals of federal officials in the Internal Revenue Service, Treasury Department and Justice Department. Senator Joseph McCarthy's Senate investigating committee provided televised coverage in 1953 and 1954 of individuals testifying with respect to espionage during and after World War II. Civil rights then dominated the domestic scene in the late 1950s and 1960s, along with a growing awareness of racial distinctions in the administration of criminal justice and a reevaluation of due process and equal protection guarantees for all persons accused of crimes.[51]

The negotiated plea was certainly not a new concept in the American criminal justice system by the 1950s, but the courts apparently were still not ready to confront the difficult question of whether its very existence should receive approval. Nevertheless, like the latest Canadian courts, U.S. courts were ready to acknowledge the practice indirectly. In *People v. Picciotti* (1958),[52] the Supreme Court of New York regulated conditions under which a negotiated guilty plea would not be considered valid. In that case, the court doubted that the guilty plea had been completely voluntary. It held that the defendant was not bound to stand by a guilty plea entered as the result of being threatened. In the court's opinion:

> A plea of guilty is, of course, frequently the result of a "bargain" but there is no bargain if the defendant is told that, if he does not plead guilty, he will suffer consequences that would otherwise not be visited upon him. To capitulate and enter a plea under a threat of an "or else" can hardly be regarded as the result of the voluntary bargaining process

between the defendant and the people sanctioned by propriety and practice.[53]

The Supreme Court agreed in *Shelton v. United States* (1958).[54] While not directly facing the question of the propriety of plea bargaining, the court vacated a conviction after an admission of error by the solicitor general, leading the court to believe that the plea of guilty may have been improperly obtained.[55]

Again in 1962, in *Machibroda v. United States* (1969),[56] the Supreme Court reiterated that "if the plea is induced by promises or threats which deprive it of its voluntary character, it is void." The unspoken implication of this case was that if the plea had been attained through negotiations free of coercion or threat, it would have been valid.

The United States Public Defender System was established to assist indigent defendants in criminal proceedings. In 1963 the landmark decision of *Gideon v. Wainwright* (1963)[57] was one of the most dramatic decisions handed down by the United States Supreme Court. "The Court declared that the Sixth Amendment right to counsel is fundamental."[58] Prior to *Gideon*, a person too poor to hire a lawyer had an unqualified constitutional right to appointed counsel in all federal court proceedings but, in state court proceedings, only when charged with a crime punishable by death. In noncapital cases in state court, the defendant had no such absolute right.[59] If forced to defend himself without a lawyer and convicted of a serious crime, he could obtain relief only if he could show specifically that he had been "prejudiced" by the absence of a lawyer, or that "special circumstances" (his lack of intelligence or education, or the gravity and complexity of the offense charged) rendered criminal proceedings without the assistance of the defense counsel "fundamentally unfair."[60] The *Gideon* court deemed it an "obvious truth" that a person "too poor to hire a lawyer cannot be assured a fair trial unless counsel is provided for him."[61] Thus, the court established an absolute right to appointed counsel in all serious criminal cases in state courts.

Most of the Warren Court's leading criminal procedure cases evoked sharp dissents on the Court and produced much unhappiness, even anger, in law enforcement circles and in the public. *Gideon* is a striking exception. It was a unanimous decision. It was supported by a broad ethical consensus. It was widely applauded by the legal profession, press and, later, a striking movie that was based on the book *Gideon's Trumpet*.

However, some say that this has come to "guarantee no more than that a person who happens to be a lawyer is presented at trial along the side of the accused." Justice Hugo L. Black, who wrote the opinion for *Gideon*, observed in another case involving the rights of indigent defendants that "there can be no equal justice where the kind of trial a man gets depends on the amount of money he has."[62]

The *Gideon* court thought it had gone a long way toward achieving "equal justice" in the administration of criminal justice. Subsequent decisions have expanded that right to other types of cases, including misdemeanors and juvenile matters, and defined the right to counsel to mean the right to effective assistance of counsel. But this expansion does not mean all is well for indigent defendants. More often than not, the quality of representation is based upon a defendant's ability to pay. Government funding for defense is low, forcing many of those who take court-appointed assignments to work for minimal fees. In practice, then, the promise of *Gideon* remains unfulfilled. Thus there appears to be a large gap between the legal services for those who can afford them and the indigents in the United States.

A latent effect of the *Gideon* decision may have been to increase the volume of plea bargaining in the United States. After *Gideon*, many state governments who otherwise would not have done so were required to implement or expand public defenders operations. As we have seen, overworked public defenders have much incentive to work out plea arrangements to dispose of cases.

In effect, since the advent of the Burger Court, the importance and legitimacy of plea bargaining have been recognized.[63] Decisions by this court continued to emphasize the voluntary nature of the plea and also indicated a willingness to move toward the formal legitimation of the plea bargaining practice.[64]

Having thus arrived at legitimacy in a round-about way, plea bargaining went on to become openly acknowledged and routinely practiced in the United States. In 1968 the American Bar Association approved a set of standards relating to guilty pleas. Rule 11(e) of the Federal Rules of Criminal Procedure was adopted in 1969 to bring the plea negotiation into the open in the federal courts.[65]

NOTES

1. Rosco Pound and Felix Frankfurter, *Criminal Justice in Cleveland: Reports of the Cleveland Foundation Survey of the Administration of Criminal Justice in Cleveland, Ohio* (Cleveland: The Cleveland Foundation, 1922).
2. First name not stated in the record.

3. Literally and in practice this means, "I am unwilling to prosecute." This motion, which has a long history, is the secret of great power in the prosecutor's office.

4. Arnold Enker, "Prospectives on Plea Bargaining," *Task Force Report: The Courts* (Washington, D.C.: U.S. Government Printing Office, 1967), 112.

5. Raymond Moley, *Politics and Criminal Prosecution* (New York: Minton, Balch, and Company, 1929), 159-64.

6. Mather, "Plea Bargaining or Trial," 141. *See also* Justin Miller, "The Compromise of Criminal Cases," *Southern California Law Review* 1 (1927): 1-2.

7. Francis Wharton, *Wharton's Criminal Evidence*, Vol. 22 (Rochester, N.Y.: Lawyers Co-operative Publishing Company, 1912), 1326.

8. Miller, "The Compromise of Criminal Cases," 22.

9. Ohlin, "Surveying Discretion," 8.

10. Moley, *Politics and Criminal Prosecution*, 661.

11. Ibid., 656.

12. Ibid., 656. *See also* David D. Van Tassel, ed., *The Encyclopedia of Cleveland History* (Bloomington, Ind.: Indiana University Press, 1987), 276.

13. Reginald Heber Smith and Herbert B. Ehrmann, *The Criminal Courts*, Part I in *The Cleveland Foundation Survey of Criminal Justice in Cleveland* (Cleveland: The Cleveland Foundation, 1921), 131.

14. Ohlin, "Surveying Discretion," 8.

15. "A Pioneer Study of Prosecution," *American Bar Association Journal* 8 (1922): 307.

16. Smith and Ehrmann, *The Criminal Courts*, 94.

17. Ibid., 96.

18. Ibid., 3-4.

19. "A Pioneer Study of Prosecution," 136.

20. Ibid.

21. Ibid., 114.

22. Ibid., 97.

23. Ibid., 99.

24. Ibid., 101.

25. Ibid., 113-14.

26. Ibid., 135.

27. Ibid., 141.

28. Ibid., 117.

29. Robert Davis, "Roscoe Pound, Felix Frankfurter, and Criminal Justice in Cleveland," *In Brief* (May 1987): 22-25.

30. Ibid., 36.

31. Alfred Bettman, *Prosecution*, Part II in *The Cleveland Foundation Survey of Criminal Justice in Cleveland* (Cleveland: The Cleveland Foundation, 1921), 230.

32. Smith and Ehrmann, *The Criminal Courts*, 95.

33. Moley, *Politics and Criminal Prosecutions*, 660.

34. *Outline of the Origin, Growth and Function of the Cleveland Association for Criminal Justice* (Cleveland: The Cleveland Association for Criminal Justice, 1921), 7.

35. Several dozen cases were cited in detail illustrative of the procedure complained of by the Association.

36. *Origin, Growth and Function*, 8.

37. Ibid., 9.

38. Ibid.

39. Ibid., 10.

40. Andrew A. Bruce, "Illinois Association for Criminal Justice Completes Crime Survey," *American Bar Association Journal* 15 (1929): 426.

41. Ibid.

42. W. F. Dodd, "Progress of Preventive Justice," *The Journal of the American Bar Association* 6 (1920): 151.

43. Edwin W. Sims, "Speedy Justice in Criminal Cases," *The Journal of the American Bar Association* 7 (1921): 598.

44. Ibid.

45. Miller, "The Compromise of Criminal Cases," 1-2.

46. Frank J. Remington, "The Decision to Charge, the Decision to Convict on a Plea of Guilty, and the Impact of Sentence Structure of Prosecution Practices," in *Discretion in Criminal Justice*, ed., Lloyd E. Ohlin and Frank J. Remington (Albany, N.Y.: State University of New York Press, 1993), 81-83.

47. Alschuler, "Plea Bargaining History," 228.

48. Ibid., 236.

49. Feeley, "Structure of the Criminal Process," 338-355.

50. Remington, "The Decision to Charge," 80. In his research, Frank Remington found that in major cities, such as Los Angeles, Cleveland, and Detroit during the 1920s and 1930s, plea bargains were used in approximately 78% to 91% of the cases. *See also* Thomas W. Church and Milton Heumann, *Speedy Disposition: Monetary Incentives and Policy Reform in Criminal Courts* (Albany, N.Y.: State University of New York Press, 1992).

51. Herbert A. Johnson, *History of Criminal Justice* (Cincinnati, Ohio: Anderson Publishing Company, 1988), 240.

52. *People v. Picciotti*, 151 N.E.2d 191 (1958).

53. Ibid.

54. *Shelton v. United States*, 356 U.S. 26 (1958).

55. Cole, *Administration of Justice*, 203.

56. *Machibroda v. United States*, 368 U.S. 487 (1969).

57. *Gideon v. Wainwright*, 372 U.S. 335 (1963).

58. Larry W. Miller, "Right to Counsel: State Courts on the Front-Line," *Annual Survey of American Law* (1984): 179.

59. Judith Kapunscinski, "Beyond 'Gideon': 25 Years Later, the Right to Counsel is not Always Assured," *The Los Angeles Daily Journal*, 1 April 1988, 4.

60. Yale Kamisar, "III. Gideon v. Wainwright: A Quarter Century Later," *Pace Law Review* 10 (1990): 349.

61. Abe Kash and Anthony Lewis. "IV. The History of *Gideon v. Wainwright*," *Pace Law Review* 1 (1990): 380.

62. Berg Martin and Dan Trigoboff, "Experts Split on Legacy of Historic High Court Ruling; *Gideon* Gets 25 Years Amidst Uncertainty for Indigents Defense; Promise or Reality?", *The Los Angeles Daily Journal*, 18 March 1980, 22.

63. *See* Gregory M. Dyer, "Criminal Defendants' Waiver of the Right to Appeal -- An Unacceptable Condition of a Negotiated Sentence or Plea Bargain," *Notre Dame Law Review* 65 (1990): 649-670.

64. *Machibroda v. United States,* 368 U.S. 487 (1962).

65. Establishing procedure for presenting the terms as was explained in greater detail in Chapter 2.

CHAPTER 7

PLEA BARGAINING IN CANADA AFTER 1920

The 1920s and 1930s were decades of turmoil and public unrest in the history of American criminal justice. Crime commissions were set up throughout the nation in an attempt to underscore the flaws in the administration of the criminal justice system. The work of these commissions resulted in a series of crime surveys from across the country which documented abuses taking place within the administration of criminal courts, police agencies and among the personnel in these institutions.

The surveys often concluded that, in the United States by the 1920s, defendants were pleading guilty in large numbers because they often had much to gain by their confessions. Unfortunately, according to commentators at the time, there were miscarriages of justice involved in many of these cases. Innocent defendants could be forced to plead guilty if convinced that their treatment would be more severe at the hands of a jury. Guilty defendants could be released after what many considered to be insufficient punishment. As such, defendants frequently hesitated to exercise their legal right to a trial for fear of prosecutorial vindictiveness, while prosecutors felt pressure to dispose of cases rather than to dispense "justice."[1]

The Canadian Archives and Oral History Collection at The Osgoode Society, in contrast, give no hint of such public distrust of the court system in Canada during this time period.[2] This is not to say that Canadians were completely oblivious to their courts or to the possibility of corruption. Nor were they unaware of abuses in courts in the United States. However, several Canadian law journals and public press articles during this period voiced concerns over the extreme laxity in the enforcement of criminal law in the States and further stated that Canadians, in contrast, saw no need to take action to examine and shake up their judicial system.[3]

Development Of Criminal Law

In the 1930s, there was little literature produced on criminal law in Canada. Furthermore, criminal law was given very little attention in Canadian law schools at that time. While there were fine textbooks on contracts and torts, there were no commensurate books on criminal law. The law review articles that appeared from time to time hardly concerned themselves with criminal issues.[4] With regard to juries, Justice Arthur G. Martin commented that:

> The juries are more sophisticated, there wasn't the exposure to the media in those days that there is now. Jurors didn't see plays or a murder case on television as they do now, and I think that they were more likely to be moved by a good performance, but I don't think the principles of good advocacy have changed.[5]

Criminal law as a field gained more importance with the creation of legal aid[6] and the eventual increase in Canadian emphasis on the protections of the individual. Such changes attracted more interest in the teaching and development of criminal law.

Important substantive changes in the development of Canadian law have occurred in Canada since 1949 when the practice of allowing appeals from Canada to the Judicial Committee of the Privy Council in England was terminated. In addition, since 1949, precedent from English appellate courts was no longer binding on Canadian courts, although such precedent was treated with respect. Since 1949, a Canadian jurisprudence has developed which is unique to its historical affiliation with English law. Moreover, particular notice has been given in Canadian jurisprudence to the legal developments in the neighboring United States.[7]

Changes Between 1950 And 1970

One of the major changes in Canadian criminal justice was the institutionalization of legal aid from a voluntary system to a statutory scheme in 1970.[8] This change, which was developed in Ontario and adopted throughout Canada, emphasized that no person should be deprived of a lawyer because of lack of financial resources. The Law Society of Upper Canada, with support by the province of Ontario, underwrote the cost of legal representation, rather than adopting a public defender's service. An accused was given the right to a lawyer of his choice based on an assessment of his financial status. The accused was provided with a certificate by the Law Society, which could be taken to hire any lawyer who was willing to take the case. According to Justice Martin, this was a very advanced system and certainly well in advance of that which existed in other countries, including the United States. This system was modeled after the legal aid system in Scotland.[9]

In 1970 Justice Martin, at the request of Chief Justice Warren E. Burger (who had recently been appointed Chief Justice of the United States), addressed the National Institute of American Bar Association at a luncheon meeting on the legal aid system in Canada. Justice Martin commented that the American attorneys were impressed with Ontario's legal aid system and wanted to learn more about it.[10] Prior to its adoption, there had been no uniformity throughout Canada. The legal aid bureau, sponsored by the Barrister's Societies, only existed in scattered urban localities. It was maintained by philanthropic or charitable institutions. The problem of the defense of indigents was primarily a concern of local societies.[11]

In addition to changes in the legal aid system, the Canadian criminal justice system in the 1960s was increasingly centralized to promote efficiency.[12] In 1967, the Ontario Attorney General assumed control from county officials of all crown attorneys in the province. In addition, in 1968, the province assumed control of all county jails.[13] These actions were undertaken to promote efficiency and homogeneity in the justice system to cope with increasing caseloads.[14]

According to Justice Martin, the system has created some problems and no doubt some abuses, but, nevertheless, those are small prices to pay for what is a unique and excellent system. The abuses are minimal since the Law Society of Upper Canada, in his view, does a tremendous job of policing the operation of the criminal justice system. According to Justice Martin, it does create more trials and longer trials, but Canadians will not tolerate people pleading guilty because they do not have the resources to hire a lawyer.

Fewer Flaws And More Frequent Preventative Measures

In Canada from the 1920s to 1950s, several commissions and committees were organized to study the administration of the criminal justice system. It appears that the efforts to set up these commissions stemmed from an ongoing effort to improve the different facets of the existing criminal justice system rather than from a perceived need to correct abuses or corruption within the system.

Issues that concerned these committees included whether the accused were being denied representation because of lack of financial resources, whether the bail system was creating injustices, and whether people were being unnecessarily held in pre-trial detention. Another area involved examining whether or not community-based corrections should be given greater priority than imprisonment. A brief review of the works of these commissions, each of which had broad authority to focus attention where it saw fit, gives a sense of the kind of issues concerning the Canadian Bar at the time, some of which evidenced a concern for sloppy or unprincipled dispensing of sentences through plea bargaining or otherwise.

The 1936 Archambault Commission

One of the first commissions to be formed was the Archambault Commission of 1936 (royal commission to investigate the penal system of Canada). It was set up to examine the Canadian correctional system in its relationship to the entire administration of criminal justice.[15] This commission presented a report positing the need for training people in the field of correction.[16] Following this, in 1947, a royal commission to revise the criminal code was appointed. In the years following the commission, the revised criminal code was enacted. Each one of these commissions had a long-term impact on the improvement of the administration of the criminal justice system in Canada, but none dealt specifically with plea bargaining. This could have been either because the practice was an informal one not outlined in Canadian criminal codes or because no revisions were felt to be necessary.

The 1941 Pre-Trial Procedure Studies

Although not a royal commission, a select committee on the administration of justice was appointed in 1941 by the Ontario Attorney General's office to look at the formal pre-trial system in the United States and to make recommendations on creating a similar system in Ontario. This committee defined the term "pre-trial procedure" as referring to a practice existing at the time in the United States. The practice was described in the reports of the Section of Judicial Administration of the American Bar Association (1938), which stated that "the purposes of the pre-trial are three-fold:

1. to narrow the issue;
2. to shorten and expedite trials; and
3. to avoid trials in cases which should not go to trial."[17]

In the United States, the formal pre-trial system existed in jurisdictions where there was a backlog of cases and a lengthy time period before cases went to trial. In many of the jurisdictions where formal pre-trial systems were adopted, the condition of the court dockets had been such that a case, upon reaching the trial list, would not have been tried for at least twelve months, and perhaps even several years. There was no doubt that pre-trial procedures were of great assistance in remedying such conditions.

The committee reported that in Ontario there were no such problems. In its opinion, any other benefits that could have been obtained from a formal pre-trial system were already present in the Canadian system of jurisprudence. This conclusion was reached by a group of judges who had thoroughly studied the pre-trial procedures in the United States.[18]

Then Registrar of the Supreme Court of Ontario, Mr. Smith, felt that formal pre-trial procedures would create another cumbersome detail which could add to the delay in getting cases tried. He had studied the pre-trial system carefully and had attended pre-trial conferences in Michigan. He believed that the Ontario system worked as well as or better than the pre-trial system in Detroit. In his opinion, the Ontario system of pleadings and discovery adequately covered everything that could have been covered in pre-trial jurisdictions.[19]

Edson Haines, who at the time headed the Ontario civil justice section of the Canadian Bar Association, also had attended formal pre-trials in Michigan. He also felt that a formal pre-trial system could not add anything to the method of trying cases in Ontario.[20] He commented that the congestion seen in many of the United States jurisdictions was not evident in the Canadian courts. He stated that if there was congestion in the court dockets, it could easily be remedied by adding extra judges and courtrooms. He further commented that the pre-trial process would only be necessary when there was a backlog of two or three years. Both lawyers and judges agreed that relieving congestion was the main purpose for pre-trials. Other advantages that could have been gained by pre-trials already were provided in the Canadian system of discovery, production of documents, and admission at trial.[21]

Various other Canadian judges who had the opportunity to observe the American system in the 1950s opined that Canadians believed in a pre-trial system as something very open and fair, whereas the American lawyer, made his admissions of pre-trial carefully and vaguely.[22] These judges felt that lawyers in Ontario were already doing what the pre-trial system was attempting to do in the United States. Photographs, pleadings, bills, etc., were all submitted to the solicitor on the other side, and judges encouraged counsel to make all admissions possible at the opening of the trial. The Canadian method of discovery, production of documents, and notice to admit, along with admissions made at trial, adequately covered all that a pre-trial system could have hoped to cover. It was the opinion of that group (judges who observed the American system) that by adding two judges in each of the court divisions, the system would come as close to perfection as would be possible in any judicial system.

THE 1953 FAUTEAUX COMMISSION ON PENAL REFORM

From the 1920s through 1950s there is little evidence of Canadian investigative commissions focusing on problems of plea bargaining abuses. Instead, most significant work involved pro-active efforts to perfect the administration of criminal justice, particularly the parole system.

In 1953 the Minister of Justice appointed a Committee of Inquiry into principles and procedures of parole service under the chairmanship of Mr. Justice Gerald Fauteaux. Its report became known as the *Fauteaux Report*,[23] and made a number of recommendations including the enactment of legislation to create a National Parole Board. On February 15, 1959, the *Parole Act* was proclaimed, transferring the authority to grant conditional release to a board with members appointed by the Governor.[24] The Report of *The Canadian Committee on Corrections Toward Unity, Criminal Justice and Corrections* (1956), led to the establishment of the National Parole Board which was responsible for reviewing all sentences imposed under the criminal law of Canada. The purpose of this system was to make those who had broken the law more responsible in their attitude toward society.[25] The Fauteaux Committee was very specific in setting high educational standards for those people who were selected to make up the first parole board.[26]

It would seem logical that a legal system concerned with its responsibility in the administration of individual justice would also have investigated pre-trial negotiations had there been a perceived problem in that area. The fact that the Fauteaux Committee was commissioned to focus only on parole and that no other committee was formed to investigate pre-trial negotiations would suggest the smooth operation of the pre-trial system.

THE 1956 YORK COUNTY COURT TRIAL COMMITTEE

The York County Court Trial Committee was appointed by the County of York Law Association in 1956 to study available measures to expedite trial process and to take the necessary steps to initiate corrective action. The purpose of this committee was to review the reasons for inadequacy of county court trial facilities. There apparently was considerable confusion in the county courts in getting matters up for trial due to an increase in the number of cases. This concern was raised when the court officials realized that they were at least three months away from a trial date at the time that an action was set for trial.

As a result of this committee's recommendation, the number of jurors and judges for the county court was increased. A new plan was instituted under which an application could be made for dates for trial, either on consent or without consent, fifteen days after entry of the action for trial.[27]

When courts in other areas experienced similar problems, the Canadian Bar Association made the same recommendation to increase the number of magistrates so that the number of cases brought before them could be reduced. This, of course, would prevent them from working under constant pressure.[28] The solution, therefore, was to increase the capacity of the system rather than to promote short-cut methods of case disposition such as extensive plea bargaining.

THE 1969 QUIMET ROYAL COMMISSION

During the first decade of the National Parole Board's existence in Canada (1959-1969), no provision was made for parole hearings. Subsequent to the recommendations of the Fauteaux Committee (1956), the Canadian Committee on Corrections (Quimet, 1969) was the first instance in which the usefulness of parole application hearing was considered.[29]

The Quimet Report demonstrated the birth of a new philosophy of leniency in the Canadian criminal justice system. This philosophy sought to inflict no greater harm on the offender than was necessary to protect society.[30]

Virtually all of the recommendations of the Quimet Committee were implemented by legislation. The Quimet Committee recommended that the criminal code should be amended to provide that all persons on arrest or detention be advised of their right to counsel, and in addition, afforded a reasonable opportunity to communicate with counsel. This principle ran through the entire recommendations of the Quimet Committee, which touched on many aspects of criminal justice.

REMEDIAL AND PREVENTIVE MEASURES BY THE PROFESSION

As previously mentioned, there is no public hint of a high level of abuse in the administration of the Canadian criminal justice system. Generally, the only evidence of undue leniency on the part of the Canadian courts is revealed in a letter to Crown attorneys from Deputy Attorney General Edward Bayly dated June 11, 1926. In this letter, Bayly pointed out that "magistrates and even county judges at times grant bail after convictions in indictable offenses." He requested that these officials follow the correct procedures and refrain from granting bail to those who were technically not entitled to it.[31] From this letter, it is apparent that local judges and magistrates were being somewhat more lenient with convicted defendants than the law strictly allowed and that the attorney general's office was aware of the practice and attempted to halt it. While there is some possibility of political pressure as a source of motivation, it appears that the criticism came from professionals within the system rather than from the pressure of outside political forces.[32]

By and large, Canadian judges have been very careful about what is printed in the popular press. According to Arthur Allison Wishart, who practiced law in Canada starting in the 1920s and later became attorney general, whenever court professionals met for issues of policymaking, a statement was always given out after the meeting.[33] In this way, the legal profession controlled what was printed instead of being influenced by it, and as such, any publicity about plea negotiations was controlled by the negotiators themselves.

Justice Carmen,[34] who was the Queen's attorney during World War II, commented that in 1945 there was an abundance of prosecution on difficult issues and, as a result, the attorney general's office had a very heavy caseload.[35] Even with a heavy caseload, the administration of justice did not get out of control as it apparently had in some American cities in earlier years.

While plea bargaining apparently did not become abused during this time period, it did continue to occur. Justice Frederick George Mackay, who was a member of the Ontario Court of Appeals until 1952, described his litigation practice. He said that he had 20 or 30 cases at any one time and that every few months during World War II, "we met and tried to settle." The Crown would hand in the statements of its side and Mackay would hand in his arguments. They talked and decided what was fair and just, then called in the clients and explained to them what would be in their best interest. In many cases, however, they disagreed and would fight those cases out in court.[36] His statement demonstrates that the cases on which they agreed as to what was fair and just were the ones which they settled by the defendant's guilty plea.

Other indications of plea bargaining can be seen from other sources. Supreme Court Justice Lieff commented on the earlier practices concerning pre-trial conferences. He stated that the idea of pre-trial conferences was conceived in many places in Canada and that widespread attention had been given to this practice in many jurisdictions. He further stated that he had looked at the practice in the federal courts in the United States, especially the District of Columbia which had a very sophisticated system of pre-trial conferences. According to Justice Lieff, "we set up [the pre-trial conferences] on an ad hoc basis with no rules, it was just a practice note that we developed and the lawyers bought it immediately, we started settling half the cases in my office and that is what it still is."[37]

THE COURTS' LACK OF CLEAR APPROVAL OF PLEA BARGAINING

While there are relatively few Canadian cases in which plea bargaining is directly discussed, it is fairly obvious that plea bargaining frequently occurred during this era.[38] For example, in *R. v. Roop* (1924)[39] the Nova Scotia Supreme Court stated that "A plea of guilty is equivalent to an admission by the accused that the prosecution could, if necessary, establish his guilt in fact and in law."[40]

In *Guerin v. R.* (1933),[41] *Brosseau v. R.*,[42] and *R. v. Dawson* (1934),[43] early 1930s cases, the courts of criminal appeals and Quebec Kings Bench voiced their concerns about voluntariness of pleas. Thus it was stated that "[C]onsequently, when it appears that the plea may have been involuntary, or when it is or may have been the result of inducements held out by a person in authority, the court will, under these circumstances, conduct an inquiry into the basis for the plea."[44]

As with the development of plea bargaining in the United States, some cases exhibited the court's concern over the treatment of the "broken bargain," a treatment which differed from court to court within Canada.[45] Two cases show this, *Rex v. Stone* (1932),[46] and *Rex v. LeBlanc*; *Rex v. Long* (1938).[47] In the first case, the defendant was charged with unlawfully hiding smuggled liquor on which duties had not been paid. She appeared before the justice, pleaded guilty, was convicted, and fined $200. She appealed to the county court which allowed the appeal to proceed, heard both sides, and quashed the conviction, having concluded that her story was truthful, including her explanation for pleading guilty. On further appeal, Justice Graham of the Nova Scotia Supreme Court, concurring with the (narrow) majority of the court, described the relevant circumstances:

> It is admitted that this defendant was promised by the prosecution that if she gave information, presumably as to who the person really was who had liquor in her garage, and pleaded guilty, the minimum fine of $50 would be imposed upon her. She gave information, which the officers however say was valueless. They therefore considered themselves absolved from their bargain; but they never told her so. They allowed her, relying on their promise, to plead guilty, and to be fined the maximum amount of $200.

Justice Graham concluded that the appeal should be dismissed:

> It may be that the bargain could not properly be made; but it was made, and was broken. In such circumstances natural justice demanded that she be given a chance to present any defense which she had, and carried the case outside the general rule that a plea of guilty is such conclusive proof of guilt that it admits of no contradiction and so bans appeal.

Justice Mellish, concurring, thought that:

> Notwithstanding her plea of guilty the defendant might well be dissatisfied with the punishment imposed and on an appeal was I think entitled at least under the peculiar circumstances of this case to plead "not guilty" and have the whole case reopened on the merits. These circumstances disclose some evidence of bargaining with her and the prosecution as to the punishment she should receive, and of her asserting her innocence and pleading guilty to protect her family.

Justice Paton, one of the dissenters, was not inclined to believe the defendant's claim of prejudice since he noted that no issue was taken on the point before the magistrate, such as a request to withdraw the plea. He also dismissed her claim to have pleaded to avoid notoriety, saying that, on the one hand, an honorable acquittal would be much preferable to a conviction, while on the other hand, she courted far more notoriety by appealing.

In this early example of the court's reaction to plea bargaining, the balance was struck by setting aside the proceedings that followed the bargain, which the Crown repudiated. The difference between the majority and the dissent may be largely due to the different evaluations they made in the effect of the inducements held out by the Crown to encourage the accused to plead guilty.

In the second case, *Rex v. LeBlanc*; *Rex v. Long* (1938),[48] both LeBlanc and Long were charged with conspiracy to commit four offenses of smuggling liquor and fraud in the avoidance of customs and excise duties. Long's trial was underway when he withdrew his plea of not guilty and pleaded guilty to a conspiracy charge punishable by seven years imprisonment. LeBlanc was arrested the same day, and pleaded guilty several days later. LeBlanc was sentenced to thirty days imprisonment plus a $1,000 fine while Long was sentenced to thirty days imprisonment plus a $500 fine. The Crown's application for leave to appeal and appeal was opposed on the ground that the Crown's counsel had made a bargain with the counsel for the accused, either as to the sentence or that no further proceedings would be taken. After considering what it termed "the extraordinary revelations" which were made before the New Brunswick Supreme Court, Chief Justice Baxter, said:

> I conclude that there was no bargain as to the charges laid out, at most, an assurance that there would be no further or other charges. It is true that Mr. Richard [Crown counsel] at times used the word "proceedings" but his general looseness in the use of language warrants me in refusing to consider that expression as applying to an appeal in this case. Sergt. Chard's affidavit makes it very clear that "charges," not "proceedings," was the term used. In any event, this was not a bargain between counsel in a civil case. Appeal did not depend upon Mr. Ramsey's intention but upon that of the Department of National Revenue. At most, if a promise were broken, it might afford some reason for this Court to say that it would not act under such circumstances. In the present case, the accused have utterly failed to show that any promise at all was made or any inducements held out before the transactions with the Magistrate with regard to the sentence were completed. Mr. Richard says there

> was no promise or undertaking by Mr. Ramsey with reference to the sentence. Owing to the peculiar developments of this appeal upon its hearing, it has become necessary for this Court to inquire whether a judicial sentence was arrived at and pronounced.[49]

He then considered the evidence of the history of the proceedings in an effort to reconstruct the events which he found disclosed bribery and perjury. Severely censuring the dishonorable conduct of both the magistrate and the defense counsel, Chief Justice Baxter recommended proper disciplinary action be taken against both. Accordingly, he concluded that the sentence was not arrived at by proper judicial consideration and should be altered to one considered adequate by the court, that is, two years and three months plus a $2,000 fine for LeBlanc and one year plus a $1,000 fine for Long.

As noted by the editors of the report, while the evidence failed to support the contention by defense counsel of a pre-sentence promise by the Crown not to appeal, the Appeal Division of the New Brunswick Supreme Court implied that had such an agreement in fact been made and broken, it might afford the court some reason to say that it would not act under such circumstances. As it was, the court found the situation scandalous and felt unencumbered in declaring a greater and proper sentence.

Canadian judges in the early part of this century at times refused to accept guilty pleas when they believed that the charges to which the defendant was pleading were less than those discovered by the facts. A rule against qualified pleas [a plea that is ambiguous] was established in 1948, stating that "It is a first 'principal' that a prisoner is not to be taken to admit an offense with which he is charged unless he pleads 'guilty' to that charge in unmistakable and unambiguous terms."[50]

In *Rex v. Dorothy Clara Soanes* (1948),[51] the Lord Chief Justice of the Criminal Court of Appeals expressed the hope that the court might state its view on what had happened in the case and what ought to happen in similar cases. When the applicant had been given charge of the jury, her counsel informed the judge that she was willing to plead guilty to infanticide, and the counsel for the Crown expressed his willingness to accept that plea. The judge refused to allow that plea to be adopted, stating that the charge ought to be tried. The judge's reason for refusing to allow acceptance of a plea of guilty of infanticide was that he could find no indication in the depositions that circumstances existed establishing the elements of infanticide, as opposed to murder.[52]

While it is impossible to lay down a hard-and-fast rule in any class of case on when a plea for a lesser offense should be accepted by counsel for the

Crown -- and it must always be in the discretion of the judge whether he will allow it to be accepted -- in the opinion of the court, where nothing appears from the depositions which can be said to reduce the crime from the more serious offense charged to some lesser offense for which a verdict may be returned, the duty of counsel for the Crown would be to present the offense charged in the indictment, leaving it as a matter for the jury, if they see it in the exercise of their undoubted prerogative, and define a verdict of guilty for the lesser offense only.[53]

In this case, the general opinion was that the judge was correct in insisting that the appellant be tried for murder. There was nothing disclosed from the depositions which would have justified a reduction of the charge from murder to infanticide and so the application for leave to appeal against conviction was refused. The Lord Chief Justice refused to accept the plea in this case because he thought it was improperly charged. The clear implication was that the prosecution, supervised by the court, should not accept a plea to any offense less than the most serious crime indicated by the facts. If the defendant would not plead guilty to that charge, the judge and jury should decide the issue. In this way, the public interest (determining the actual guilt and then sentencing with that guilt in mind, rather than sentencing on two lawyers behind the scenes arguing as to guilt) would be met.[54]

Even though these Canadian cases address the practice of plea bargaining, the Canadian courts in this era did not explicitly endorse or approve of the practice, nor did they abolish it. Throughout the early part of the twentieth century it seems that Canadians expressed relatively few concerns over the administration of criminal justice in Canada. Some of the problems which did arise were similar, though perhaps to a lesser degree, to those of their southern neighbors; for example, judges being overworked, heavy caseloads, the lack of resources, and the lack of trained personnel in the area of corrections.[55] As seen throughout this chapter, however, it does not appear that the Canadian Bar and judiciary fell victim to the same breakdown and possible corruption of the criminal justice system as experienced by their American counterparts.

Notes

1. *See* Heumann, *Prosecutors, Judges and Defense Attorneys.*
2. Oral History Collection of the Osgoode Society of Upper Canada, Attorney General's Record RG-4-02, Ontario Archives, Toronto, Ontario.
3. "Criminal Statistics in Anglo-Saxon Countries," 368.
4. Martin, interview by Mrs. C.J.N. Kates.

5. Martin, interview.

6. John C. Weaver, *Crimes, Constables, and Courts: Order and Transgression in a Canadian City, 1816-1970* (Montreal: McGill-Queen's University Press, 1995), 162-163.

7. *See* Gordon Glendon, *Comparative Legal Traditions: Text, Materials and Cases on the Civil Law, Common Law and Socialist Law Traditions* (St. Paul, Minn.: West Publishing Company, 1985).

8. Weaver, *Crimes, Constables, and Courts*, 162-163.

9. Martin, interview by Mrs. C.J.N. Kates.

10. Ibid.

11. Canadian Bar Association, Administration of Criminal Justice Section, "Criminal Report," Attorney General's Record RG 4-02, Ontario Archives, Toronto, Ontario, 1956.

12. Weaver, *Crimes, Constables, and Courts*, 270.

13. Ibid.

14. Ibid.

15. Martin, interview by Mrs. C.J.N. Kates.

16. Ontario Department of Attorney General, "Education in the Correctional Field," Memorandum, June 16, 1959, Attorney General's Record RGH-02, Ontario Archives, Toronto, Ontario.

17. Robert A. Kelso, Memorandum, Attorney General, June 1956, Attorney General's Record RG 4-32, Ontario Archives, Toronto, Ontario.

18. Ibid. Interviews with Justice F.G. Mackay, Judge of the Appellate Division; Justice Carl Stewart, Judge of the Supreme Court of Ontario; Gordon Reddes, Deputy Registrar of the Supreme Court of Ontario; William Vaukhall, Registrar of the County Court of the County of New York.

19. Kelso, Memorandum, 3.

20. Ibid., 4.

21. Ibid.

22. Ibid.

23. *Fauteaux Report* (Ottawa: Queen's Printer, 1956).

24. Parole is a procedure which is designed to be a logical step in the reformation and rehabilitation of offenders. *See Fauteaux Report*, 51.

25. "Helping to Reduce Crime," *The Kingston Whig Standard*, 14 May 1958, Office of the Legislative Assembly, R.G. 49, Press Clippings Service.

26. Martin, interview by Mrs. C.J.N. Kates.

27. J. F. McGarry to Robert A. Kelso, Attorney General, June 16, 1956, Ontario Attorney General's File RG 4-32, Ontario Archives, Toronto, Ontario.

28. W. B. Common, Minutes of a meeting of counsel of the Canadian Bar Association, Chateau Frontenac, Quebec, September 9, 1960, Attorney General's Record RG-4-02, Ontario Archives, Toronto, Ontario.

29. *Quimet Committee Report* (Ottawa: Queen's Printer, 1969), 329.

30. Martin, interview by Mrs. C.J.N. Kates.

31. Circular letter to Crown attorneys regarding judges and magistrates granting bail after conviction, 1926, *Ministry of Attorney General Series RG 4-32*, 1956.

32. "Plan fall legislation to tighten measures on granting bail," Attorney General's Record RG-4-02, Ontario Archives, Toronto, Ontario; Department of the Attorney General, Criminal appeals, February 18, 1957, Attorney General's Record RG 4-02, Ontario Archives, Toronto, Ontario; W. H. Price, Attorney General of Ontario, broadcast over CKNC on crime prevention, December 6, 1932, Attorney General Series RG 4-32, Ontario Archives, Toronto, Ontario.

33. Oral History Collection, Osgoode Society of Upper Canada, tape recording, December 14, 1986, Ontario Archives, Toronto, Ontario.

34. First name not stated in the record.

35. Justice Carmen, interview by Mrs. C.J.N. Kates, October 29, 1979, Oral History Collection, Osgoode Society of Upper Canada, Toronto, Ontario.

36. Justice Frederick George Mackay, Judge of the Appellate Division, Oral History Collection, Osgoode Society of Upper Canada, tape recording, December 14, 1986, Ontario Archives, Toronto, Ontario.

37. Justice Abraham Herman Lieff, Supreme Court Justice, interview by Mrs. C.J.N. Kates, March 3, 1978, Oral History Collection, Osgoode Society of Upper Canada, Ontario Archives, Toronto, Ontario.

38. Ferguson and Roberts, "Directions for Canadian Reform," 501.

39. 426*R. v. Roop*, 57 N.S.R. 325, 42 C.C.C. 344 (1924).

40. Grosman, *Exercise of Discretion*, 29.

41. *Guerin v. R.*, 55 Que. K.B. 84, 60 C.C. 350 (1933).

42. *Brosseau v. R.*, 3 C.C.C. 129 (1934).

43. *R. v. Dawson*, 18 Cr. App. R. 111 (1934).

44. Ibid.

45. Bettman, *Prosecution*, 502.

46. *Rex v. Stone*, 58 C.C.C. 262 (1932).

47. *Rex v. LeBlanc & Long*, 71 C.C.C. 232 (1938).

48. Ibid.

49. Ibid.

50. A. E. Popple, "Accepting a Plea of Guilty," C.R. 1 (1946): 183.

51. *Rex v. Dorothy Clara Soanes*, 32 C.A.R. 136 (1948).

52. Ibid.

53. Ibid.

54. Anthony Davis, "Sentences for Sale: A New Look at Plea Bargaining in England and America," *Criminal Law Review* (1971): 150.

55. Committee on the Reform of the Administration of Justice, Proceedings of a meeting held in Toronto, Ontario, October 3, 1956, Attorney General's Record RG-4-02, Ontario Archives, Toronto, Ontario.

CHAPTER 8
CONCLUSION

After witnessing more than one hundred plea bargaining sessions in the United States and Canada, after interviewing and getting to know lawyers for both the prosecution and the defense in both countries, and after studying their laws and history, I have developed strongly held views about the day-to-day dispensing of "justice" in these neighboring countries. The most important of these is my observation of the difference between the rhetoric of the law and the actual operation of the legal system.

It is sometimes thought that the United States and Canada are twins born of a common parent, the United Kingdom. An examination of these nations' criminal justice systems, however, tells a different story. While they have a common parent, they experienced quite different births. As a result, the United States' Constitution and legal tenants espouse the protection of individual rights against incursion by the government. Canadian legal history demonstrates less emphasis on individual rights, both in the enacted legislation and in the rhetoric of the law. Although the court systems in Canada and the United States mirror the English system to some degree, nevertheless, "there is a very persistent and significant differences in Canadian and American attitudes toward issues of due process and crime control."[1]

What is the reality of these differences? Lipset has suggested that the lower rates of crime and violence in Canada are accompanied by greater respect for police and by public support for stronger punishment of criminals.[2] As somewhat of a contrast to this, the Fifth Amendment of the Constitution of the United States provides the sweeping assurance that "no person . . . shall be deprived of life, liberty, or property, without due process of law." This has come to mean, among other things, that a defendant not only has a right to a trial by jury, but that it must be a "fair" trial in a variety of respects.[3] Other amendments, including the Fourth, the Sixth, the Fourteenth, and other provisions of the Fifth Amendment, augment those individual guarantees by prohibiting certain kinds of searches and seizures, by guaranteeing a right to trial by jury, by protecting an accused's prerogative to remain silent and by providing other procedural safeguards. By all outward indications of stated principles, the U.S. justice system is more focussed on protection of individual "due process", and less on "crime control", than the Canadian system. This mirrors the view expressed by Hagan and Leon.

At the same time, the formal system in both countries is adversarial in nature. The law provides for both a prosecutor who will present the state's case and a defense attorney who will defend the accused by challenging the state's case. Yet, the majority of defendants in both countries trade away their right to a fair trial and, instead, enter a plea of guilty to a negotiated charge. Any realistic analysis of these two criminal justice systems *must* come to grips with this major ingredient.

A close examination of plea bargaining raises a conflict between the philosophical rhetoric and the practical realities of day-to-day existence. There is a significant ideological disparity, for example, between American legal ideals of constitutional "due process" and the day-to-day practice of plea negotiations.

As indicated in Chapter 1, one purpose of this book has been to examine the distinction noted by Hagan and Leon between the criminal justice systems of the United States and Canada. The amount of discretion and its manner of use is a central factor. As Rosco Pound wrote in 1956, in a contemporary criminal justice system there is an inherent need for discretionary decision-making to be exercised at one or more points in the system:

> Throughout legal history there has been a movement back and forth between rule and discretion in the judicial process . . . discretion in the administration of justice was sought to be, if not eliminated, at any rate held to the narrowest limits. *In criminal justice especially it was felt dangerous to allow the judge to act otherwise than within the well defined limits of rules.* But the general bigness of everything, the shift from an agricultural to an industrial society, the growth of huge metropolitan centers, the rise of the welfare or service state, and the consequent demand for administrative agencies and individualized

> application of law to multiplying and unforeseen conditions, have been compelling recognition of discretion as an inevitable and essential element in adjudication, to be exercised within legal limits and on principles of reason, yet not to be excluded or held down so as to preclude individualization peculiarly needed in penal administration.[4]

In terms of Packer's paradigm, a system tending toward the "crime control" model vests a large measure of discretion in the hands of the police, prosecutors and judges, while a system tending toward the "due process" model seeks to limit and restrict that discretion in order to guard the rights of the individual.

The effect of plea bargaining on the criminal justice process obviously depends on what one means by that term, and on what is to be accepted as part of the practice. Where it is carried out to clarify the facts of the case in the minds of the prosecutor/Crown and defense counsel, and to present to an impartial and uninvolved judge a reasonable summary of the case and a joint recommendation of a range of sentence, it would appear to facilitate the smooth functioning of the system with relatively little exercise of discretion and, coincidentally, little risk to the accused that his freedom will be trampled in the process. When the bargain involves free-wheeling trade-offs among the judge, defense and prosecution, the criticisms of the bargaining process abound. In such cases, the broad discretion exercised to negotiate the plea is disturbing due to the potential for unfair or unprincipled deals which, in the case of well-represented offenders, may be too lenient, or in the case of naive offenders, may be too harsh.[5] Where the discretion is wide, plea bargaining is influenced by many intangible elements, such as the quality of the relationship between the defense lawyer and the prosecutor or Crown, and the cooperation between the suspect and the police.

Even though the practice has become accepted, plea bargaining seems to make Canadians legal professionals generally uncomfortable. This discomfort is reflected in the reluctance of judges, defense attorneys and Crown attorneys in even talking about it. This apprehension appears to me to have kept the exercise of discretion narrowly circumscribed.

Years ago, legal professionals in the United States also treated plea bargaining with such concern. At one time, an American Bar Association committee considered the possibility of revising United States practices in a manner more like the Canadian practice by withdrawing the judge from all phases of the guilty plea, and merely permitting him to accept or reject the recommendation of the prosecutor (without any advance indication of his probable action). Similarly, many legal scholars over the years have opposed the practice of plea bargaining. Rosco Pound, Raymond Moley, and others associated with the crime surveys of the 1920's stressed the risk it presented for political influence as a factor in the administration of justice. Nonetheless, reforms such as the American Bar Association proposal ultimately were rejected because: (1) many states elect their judges, and with the prosecutor a likely candidate in opposition for the judgeship, friction might develop; (2) post-conviction relief would be sought by any defendant who is given a harsher sentence than recommended; and (3) the negotiated plea of guilty would be largely nullified as any defendant would want to be reasonably assured that the judge would follow the negotiated recommendation.[6]

How is it that the legal profession in the United States developed a set of attitudes more accepting of plea bargaining, since, according to Heumann, lawyers are hostile toward plea negotiations when they first finish law school?[7] Under the pressures generated by crime in an urban society, the practice today has become widely approved, institutionalized and legitimized by the American Bar Association and the U.S. Supreme Court. The current acceptance of plea bargaining in the United States also extends to legal scholars. It seems that the current emphasis of legal scholars is to establish guidelines, on the theory that doing so will eliminate abuses of plea bargaining. This widespread open acceptance, in my opinion, has led to a sometimes cavalier and jaded attitude and to wide-ranging exercise of discretion in plea bargaining among some participants in the United States criminal justice system.

We have seen that through the history of American criminal justice the need for the broad discretion of free-wheeling plea bargaining has been justified on two counts: resources and the desire for individualized justice. This raises many questions, however. Was the practice perceived to have gotten out of hand such that there was a need for a set of formal standards to control it? Or were those standards adopted to give the aura of due process in the administration of criminal justice in the plea bargaining arena? Does this practice promote well-reasoned individualized justice? Or does it merely promote efficiency? How could a system that relies ninety percent of the time on guilty pleas as a method of case disposition promote due process rights of the accused defendants? What does the manner in which Canada and the United States carry out plea bargaining tell us about the "crime control" versus "due process" tendencies posited by Hagan and Leon?

In the United States, the reality of criminal proceedings, in my experience, is different than the rhetoric.[8] Cases involving contested issues of due process are rare. Instead, the system has evolved to a state in which expediency is the principal goal, and broad discretion on the part of the participants to cut a deal is the means of achieving that goal. Ironically, the dominant method of case disposition, plea bargaining, thereby exhibits characteristics of Packer's crime control model, rather than the due process model.

The Canadian system, at least in its implementation of plea negotiations, is more like Packer's due process model in that the exercise of discretion is more constrained and there is less concern about expediency and more concern about ensuring that the facts and law match the conviction and sentence. The Canadian system, which ostensibly puts less emphasis on individual rights, in reality may provide greater protection in an average case than the real-life procedures at work in the U.S. system.

Despite all of its proclamations of protecting the individual's due process rights against the tyranny of the state, the average defendant charged with a crime in the United States (i.e., those who can not afford a high-powered defense) is subjected to a process that easily can compromise those principles of due process and equal protection. Thus, the reality of the society's rules in this arena differ from the rhetoric. This conclusion, arrived at by taking plea bargaining into account, contradicts the characterization found in other comparative studies of the United States and Canadian criminal justice systems.

Putting Packer's conceptual models aside, the more interesting question is this -- what does this comparison of the United States and Canadian systems suggest regarding future policy choices? For some time now, state and federal governments in the United States have been engaged in a "war on crime" -- an open acknowledgment that something must be done about the level of criminal behavior. At this moment in history, Canada has a better record. If we assume that the operation of a nation's criminal justice system has some influence on the level of crime in that society[9], then one must wonder if the United States can take a lesson from Canada. If so, what would it be?

The three potential objectives of criminal punishment are retribution, rehabilitation and deterrence. When it comes to retribution, it would seem that the Canadian system produces a more satisfactory result, since, even in the area of plea negotiation, there is a concerted effort among the participants to see that a uniform and consistent measure of sanction is applied to the detected criminal activity. Thus, even-handed retribution is more likely to occur. The same can be said about the deterrence objective. Would-be criminals presumably are more likely to be deterred by the knowledge that rules of law will be applied without exception than by the knowledge that the system varies widely, depending on how the game is played. Regarding rehabilitation, it is difficult to say whether a more random system for distribution of criminal sanctions, as found in the United States, is better or worse for a rehabilitation. One could argue, however, that both in the case of deterrence and rehabilitation, a uniform system is preferred because it tends to promote respect for the rules of an organized society, while a more random system promotes cynicism and disrespect for the law among fringe elements of society, among criminals, among members of the Bar and Judiciary, and among the public at-large. Indeed, this is the basis on which many oppose plea bargaining since, in their view, "justice" should not be -- and should not be *seen* to be -- something that can be negotiated at the bargaining table. All of these arguments militate towards reducing the range of discretion exercised in plea bargaining.

A reduction in the range of discretion can be accomplished in several ways. One obvious way is for the people in the United States to more consistently elect "law and order" judges and prosecutors and establish watchdog agencies to publish information which would alert an otherwise uninformed public of abuses and enable them to replace the faulty officials at the next election. This would be consistent with traditional notions of democratic self-government. But it has some obvious problems, such as the need for resources to carry it out and the difficulty of getting the message through to the electorate.

Another solution, already adopted to some degree, is the establishment of mandatory sentencing guidelines. This also has its problems, such as the ability of the prosecutor and judge to tailor the crime charged to fit the negotiated sentence, and the possibility of forcing undeserved harsh treatment in some instances.

The third alternative is to replace the elected prosecutors and judiciary with appointed officials, as is done in the U.K. or Canada. At present, discretion in the United States often is with elected prosecutors and elected judges who may not necessarily have high-minded philosophical notions of "justice" as their top priority. In contrast, their Canadian counterparts are insulated from such political pressures and are indoctrinated through years of "articling" and similar screening to develop a strong belief in their duty as guardians of society. Oddly enough, the greatest protection of individual rights and the dignity of an organized society may come from placing discretion in the hands of an insular elite group such as this, rather than elected officials. This insulation could allow discretion to remain distributed among those best situated to use it but, at the same time, would tend to ensure that those who have it are constrained by deeply instilled beliefs against using it in ways that denigrate the system. Unfortunately, the United States' historical roots of revolution, individualism and anti-elitism, all of which are manifest in the laws and constitutions of the country, are at odds with this idea.

NOTES

1. Hagan and Leon, "The Rehabilitation of Law," 248.

2. Lipset, "The Cultural Dimension," 131.

3. Loftus E. Becker, Jr., "Plea Bargaining and the Supreme Court," *Loyola of Los Angeles Law Review* 21 (April 1988): 763.

4. Rosco Pound, introduction to *Crime, Courts and Probation*, by Charles Lionel Chote and Marjorie Bell (New York: The Macmillan Company, 1956).

5. As demonstrated in Chapters 2 and 3.

6. American Bar Association, *Project on Minimum Standards*, 37-52.

7. *See* Heumann, *Prosecutors, Judges and Defense Attorneys.*

8. Other social commentators recently have made the same observations. Michael Kinsley, "TRB From Washington: Inadmissible," *The New Republic*, 6 May 1991.

9. That is, if we assume that the presence or absence of criminal behavior is not so heavily dominated by other societal factors as to make the operation of the criminal justice system irrelevant.

APPENDIX A: CANADIAN COURT CASES

52. *R. v. Agozzino et al.*, 1 C.C.C. 380, 381 (1970).
The magistrate imposed a two-year suspended sentence, with probation to keep the peace for the same time, plus a fine of $2,500 following a plea of guilty on a charge of possession of counterfeit money. In discussing sentence he said, among other things: "If the Crown attorney had not said he was not seeking a jail term . . ." (which was so), and then continued in such a way as to indicate that but for that position taken by the Crown attorney a jail term would have been imposed.

> On appeal by the Crown, Chief Justice Gale, for the court, said that it agreed with the Crown's first position that the sentence imposed was utterly inadequate for the gravity of the offense. However, the court merely altered the sentence to add one day in jail, thereby giving effect to the Crown's second submission that the imposition of a fine following a suspended sentence was illegal.

He further explained:

> We make this variation because prior to the trial Crown counsel intimated that he would not ask for a jail term and on the basis of such intimation counsel for the accused received instructions to plead guilty. There is evidence before us to indicate that had it not been for the position taken by the Crown which was subsequently adopted by the Magistrate, the accused would not have pleaded guilty. The circumstances, therefore, dictate a dismissal of the Crown's appeal as to sentence even though, had we thought ourselves at liberty to consider its propriety, we probably would have come to a different conclusion. Crown counsel at the trial represented the Attorney General. He declared that he was not seeking a jail term, whereupon the accused and his counsel made a major decision as to how the trial should be approached. The imposition of a term of imprisonment of one day in effect carries out the burden of the Crown's submission as to sentence and at the same time removes any question as to its technical accuracy. We believe it would now be quite unfair, not only to the Magistrate but to the accused, for the Crown, by means of this appeal, to change its position by asking for a substantial term of imprisonment. In effect the appeal repudiates the position taken by Crown counsel at the trial and we do not care to give effect to that repudiation.

58. *R. v. Brown*, 8 C.C.C. (2d) 227 (O.C.A. 1972).
The accused appealed from the sentence imposed following his conviction for possession of a stolen motorcycle. It is simplest to quote Chief Justice Gale, who once again delivered the court's judgment:

> It is perfectly clear that prior to the commencement of the trial, counsel for the appellant and counsel for the Crown agreed that if the latter would withdraw the theft charge, and all other outstanding charges other than the possession charge, and would make representations to the trial judge that he was not asking that any sentence imposed in this case be consecutive to a sentence of six months which the appellant was then serving, the appellant would plead guilty to the possession of charge. The appellant pleaded but, on the whole, seems to have urged the trial judge, who, of course, was not in any way bound, and perhaps knew nothing of the prior arrangement, to impose a consecutive term. In the result, the trial judge sentenced the appellant to nine months definite and six months indeterminate, consecutive to the six-month sentence then being served.
>
> We are all of the view that in the circumstances the appeal against sentence ought to be allowed, and the sentence changed to a concurrent term.

59. *Attorney General of Canada v. Roy*, 18 C.R.N.S. 89 (Que.Q.B 1972). The Crown appealed against the sentence of a fine of $150 following the accused's plea of guilty to a charge of unlawfully manufacturing spirits contrary to The Excise Tax Act. The sentence imposed by the summary conviction court had been suggested by counsel who then appeared for the Crown. Upon appeal Crown sought a fine of $500 instead on the basis that its suggestion at trial was made by mistake and the sentence was inadequate.

> The appeal raised the issue of the propriety of plea bargaining and of the role of Crown counsel in the fixing of sentences. It is clear that this case was an example of a sentence negotiated and arrived at by consent prior to the plea, so that, as in *Agozzino*, it was somewhat predicated upon the prior intimation by counsel for the Crown as to the nature of the penalty which would be sought. After noting as well the cases of *Turner* and *Kirkpatrick* (below), Mr. Justice Hugessen pronounced these principles:

> 1. Plea bargaining is not to be regarded with favor. In the imposition of sentence the court, whether in first instance or in appeal, is not bound by the suggestions made by Crown counsel.
>
> 2. Where there has been a plea of guilty and Crown counsel recommends a sentence, a court, before accepting the plea, should satisfy itself that the accused fully understands that his fate is, within the limits set by law, in the discretion of the judge, and that the latter is not bound by the suggestions or opinions of Crown counsel. If the accused does not understand this, the guilty plea ought not to be accepted.

He held that, under all the circumstances, the Crown did not satisfy the foregoing test, and dismissed the appeal with this advice:

> The Crown may feel that it has made a bad bargain, but the solution to that must surely be for the Crown to make no bargains at all. If it had declined to do so in the present case it would not have been in the position in which it now finds itself.

60. *R. v. Wood*, 26 C.C.C. (2d) 100 (Atla.A.C., App. Div. 1975).
The accused was charged with gross indecency, but having elected to be tried by a judge and jury, re-elected before a provincial court judge to plead guilty to count one whereupon count two was withdrawn. He was sentenced to probation for 30 months. The Crown applied for leave to appeal. Defense counsel raised the question as to whether the Crown should be allowed to appeal since it had been intimated to the provincial court judge that it was not seeking a jail sentence.

McDermid, J.A., first considered the fitness of the sentence in accordance with its obligation under Section 614 of the *Criminal Code* and concluded that a prison sentence was required and that his viewpoint was supported by the Fourth Annual Report of The Law Reform Commission of Canada and the authors of "Plea Bargaining: Directions for Canadian Reform" (infra), he said that in his:

> opinion, a Judge should take no part in any discussion as to sentencing before a plea has been taken, and all the circumstances in regard to the particular case have been placed before him, then having listened to the submission of counsel he should give his decision. The Provincial

Judge was quite right in the attitude he took and Crown counsel was quite wrong in saying he had no objection to such a discussion on behalf of the Crown. For a Judge in Alberta to take any part in what has been called "plea bargaining" is, in my opinion, quite improper.

He next considered whether the Crown should be allowed to change its position, to the alleged prejudice of the accused who pleaded guilty in reliance upon it, from that of not seeking a jail sentence. He considered *Agozzino, Brown*. Preferring the Crown not to make a submission to the judge as to sentence unless requested, he commented upon the danger of the attorney general not agreeing with a sentence particularly recommended by the Crown and accordingly imposed by the court. However, he would not confine the attorney general's right of appeal to that position but regarded it simply as circumstance to be taken into consideration in discharging the duty of the court to "consider the fitness of the sentence appealed against." McDermid, J.A.'s remedy could have been to grant a new trial; to avoid unfairness to the accused, the Crown would be barred from introducing as evidence the accused's previous plea of guilty.

Agreeing with McDermid, J.A., in principle, Moir, J.A. (Haddad, J.A. concurring), said that in determining whether or not leave to appeal should be granted, the court seeks to ensure fair play, and noted that the accused could be prejudiced in ways other than the admission against him of a guilty plea, as well as the factual prejudice of the change of penalty after the lengthy period since sentencing. Thus, he refused leave to appeal because the accused could not be restored to his pre-plea position and because of the delay.

62. *Perkins & Pigeau v. The Queen*, 35 C.R.N.S. 222 (Que.C.A. 1976).

The accused had been charged with illegal importing under N.C.A. section 5(2) and with possession for the purpose of trafficking contrary to N.C.A. section 4(1). The Crown accepted their pleas to the second count and joined in a submission with the defense for a sentence of 3 years imprisonment, explaining to the trial judge that this was normal and that the federal Crown was following a policy of reducing these charges, as was done here, even though it could prove them and wanted the court to continue to regard it as an importation case. The trial judge imposed sentences of 4 years, against which the defense appealed.

For the court, Rinfret gave reasons dismissing the appeal. Obviously critical of the perceived submission of this part of the law by the policy of the Department of Justice, he considered the practice of "plea bargaining" unacceptable, whether the initiative for it came from the Crown or the defense.

63. *Regina v. Roy*, 32 C.C.C. (2d) 97 (O.C.A. 1976).

The accused was charged with 2 counts and eventually tried in county court judges' criminal court and convicted on the second, willfully setting fire. During the trial, the judge called counsel into his chambers where he initiated discussions respecting a possible plea of guilty to a lesser offense by the accused. After consultation with his client, defense counsel advised he was denying that he was the one who committed the offense, and the case continued although the accused did not testify with the result noted above. He was sentenced to 3 months imprisonment plus 2 years probation. His appeal from conviction was allowed on the ground that because of what transpired during the trial it could not be said that justice appeared to have been done. A new trial with a jury was granted.

In his oral judgment for the court, Brooke, J.A., said:

> A Judge conducting a trial without the intervention of a jury is of course the trier of fact and determines the question of guilt or innocence. In my opinion he cannot initiate such a discussion after entering upon the trial and hearing evidence and still preserve the appearance of impartiality and being of an open mind, which qualities are so essential to a fair trial and the meaning of the presumption of innocence. The fact that he initiates such a discussion and sends counsel to the accused with talk of pleas of guilty and terms of sentence could reasonably result in apprehension by the accused that the Judge presiding at his trial had reached some conclusions about the case. It does not hurt to repeat again that justice must appear to be done. This is not limited simply to what is seen from the floor of the courtroom or by the public but includes what transpired here. It is also vital that justice must appear to be done, to the accused man in particular. In those circumstances we think the trial lacked this quality and therefore it cannot stand.

64. *Her Majesty the Queen v. Daniel Charles Talbot* (unreported case, no. 454/76, of the O.C.A. released Dec. 14, 1976, Houldon, Martin & Blair, J.J.A.).

The accused pleaded guilty to a charge of possession of a weapon for the purpose of committing an offence and was sentenced to 3= years of imprisonment, against which he appealed on the basis of his confusion when he pleaded and his denial of knowledge of his co-accused's possessing the weapon. Prior to pleading guilty, counsel for the Crown and the accused (two -- including the co-accused) saw the trial judge in his chambers where they discussed the plea of guilty and the range of sentence. Counsel for the co-accused suggested an appropriate range for him was 5 years and counsel for the accused suggested four years was an appropriate range for him. The trial judge imposed three years sentence since the accused had already spent six months in custody. The appeals court concluded that the accused had not suffered any prejudice from his plea of guilty and the sentence that was imposed, so the appeal was dismissed.

In accepting the plea of guilty, the discussion that had taken place in chambers were revealed in open court and recorded in the transcript. The appellant was represented by competent counsel. Crown counsel did not deviate from the arrangement concerning sentence that he had discussed with the judge in chambers. The trial judge was careful to outline to the appellant the nature and consequence of his plea of guilty. The plea of guilty was made without pressure.

65. *Regina v. Arthur*, 39 C.C.C. (2d) 158 (P.E.I.S.C., App.Div. 1978).

Considering the cases of *Agozzino*, *Roy* (1972), *Wood*, *Brown*, and *Turner*, MacDonald, J., said that it was permissible for the Crown to make a sentence submission, silence as to which wastes the Court's time if it immediately appeals an unsatisfactory sentence. However, the recommendation of a particular sentence may make it difficult for that stand to be repudiated on appeal, which is what he said the Crown now sought to do.

Finding that the sentence was neither illegal, nor that the Crown was misled, he said any verification of the sentence must be on the ground that it was grossly insufficient and that such a variation was in the public interest. Although he, as trial judge, would probably have imposed a jail term, he concluded:

> However, I must weigh the fact that the respondent has entered a guilty plea and that it is now too late for him to ask for leave to change his plea. His guilty plea was entered on the understanding that the Crown would not speak on sentencing and I do not feel it would be fair to the respondent to sentence him when he may well have entered a not guilty plea had he known a jail sentence was being sought by the Crown. While this case is very close to being one where the gravity of the crime

outweighs the public interest in the administration of justice, the benefit must be given to the accused. As was said by Hugessen, J., in the Roy case [at 93]: "The Crown may feel that it made a bad bargain, but the solution to that must surely be for the Crown to make no bargains at all."

As the accused cannot be put back in the position he was before he entered the guilty plea, I would refuse leave to appeal.

66. *Regina v. Ferrio & Richards* (reported in Crowns Newsletter, April 1979, p. 39, Ont.Co.Ct., April 3, 1979).

The accused was charged with possession of cannabis marijuana for the purpose of trafficking and with possession of cocaine for the purpose of trafficking. A preliminary inquiry was waived, the accused having elected to be tried by judge without a jury. After numerous adjournments, the case came before Her Honor Judge Dymond for trial at which time a motion before arraignment to stay the indictment for abuse of process was brought on the basis of a plea bargain having been made in the provincial court with the Crown. After hearing evidence from one defense counsel, two police officers and four Crown attorneys, Her Honor concluded that an agreement was entered into by defense counsel with the federal prosecutors' office that the accused would plead guilty to possession of cocaine only, and that the Crown would not make representation for a custodial sentence. It was probable that in the turmoil of a normal provincial court day, the federal prosecutor forgot about the agreement and did not make any note of it. This agreement was reached before the waiver of evidence and the election of trial by judge alone. Her Honor made these findings in case she erred on the legal issue of her jurisdiction, of which she held she had none, to stay the proceedings even if there were an abuse of process. Thus, she disposed of the argument that the accused would be prejudiced by having given up the right to a jury trial by the representations of the Crown by accepting the Crown's undertaking to consent to a re-election. Likewise, she rejected a second argument based on *Agozzino* and *Roy* (1972) (of a sort of "estoppel") by distinguishing those cases as applicable only after a plea or other irrevocable step by the accused relying on the position taken by the Crown. In the circumstances it was not necessary to consider the legality of the proposed sentence nor the gravity of the offense. Finally, observing that there was not a scintilla of evidence that the defense misled the Crown, Her Honor expressed her abhorrence of the repudiation by the Crown of its position taken while the case was before the provincial court and the communication of that repudiation to defense counsel more than a year later.

68. *Regina v. Johnston & Tremayne*, 4 C.C.C. 64 (O.C.A. 1970).

Johnston and Tremayne were both charged with conspiracy to import a narcotic and with possession for the purpose of trafficking. Johnston pleaded guilty to the first count, Tremayne the second and the alternative count in each case was dismissed without evidence being offered by the Crown on it. Each was sentenced to 14 years imprisonment and sought leave to appeal.

Gale, C.J.O., in his decision on behalf of the court, noted that:

> After the accused pleaded guilty, a circumstance which is of some significance, counsel for the Crown before the learned trial Judge, agreed with the recommendation offered by counsel for the accused respectively that their sentences should be five years and seven years. The learned Judge, of course, was not bound to act on it on the hearing of this appeal. It is perfectly obvious that the learned Judge took the view that the recommendation which had been made was not appropriate and he imposed what I think might well be looked upon as maximum terms having regard to the fact that it was marijuana and not one of the more insidious drugs which was being imported and handled.

Due to the effect the court felt ought to have been given to the pleas of guilty as well as background and character information not presented to the trial judge, the sentences were reduced to 10 and 7 years for Johnston and Tremayne, respectively.

71. *Her Majesty the Queen v. Kirkpatrick*, Que.C.A. 337 (1971).

The accused pleaded guilty to a charge of break and enter with intent to commit theft. His counsel suggested that the trial judge impose a fine of $1,000 and place him on probation for 2 years. Upon being asked by the judge for his comments, the Crown attorney replied that they had no objections to a fine of $1,000. The accused was sentenced to one day in jail plus a $1,000 fine plus 3 years probation. The Crown appealed.

The majority of the court, while lamenting the repudiation by the Crown of its position, nevertheless considered that the facts called for a more severe sentence, of 3 years penitentiary. The dissenting judges would have dismissed the appeal, observing that in the circumstances there was no urgent public interest to justify the repudiation by the Crown of a position taken by its representative in charge of the case since that is derogatory to the orderly administration of justice.

72. *Regina v. Mouffe*, 16 C.R.N.S. 257 (Que.C.A. 1971).
The accused pleaded guilty to a charge of robbery and was sentenced to 6 months imprisonment. The third ground of the appeal by the Crown against the sentence was that "the trial judge did not give sufficient weight to the representations put forth by the Crown." The trial judge's report explained that it was solely upon the basis of the recommendations of counsel for the Crown, who had said he was satisfied with a sentence of 6 months, that he imposed the sentence in question. Rinfret, J.A., held that counsel for the Crown was clearly entitled to suggest a sentence but it was the prerogative of the court to accept or reject such suggestion. The appeal was allowed and 4 years imprisonment substituted. Tremblay, C.J.Q., concurred, as did Casey, J.A., who added that:

> . . it is the duty of the Crown to supply the Court with whatever information it requires for the purpose of sentence. But there it ends and the fact that the Crown suggests the sentence does not relieve this Court of its duty to intervene if such sentence is incompatible with the prime purpose of punishment.

As he did in *Kirkpatrick*, Montgomery, J.A., (Turgeon, J.A., concurring) dissented, saying that:

> In my opinion, it is derogatory to the orderly administration of justice that the Crown should repudiate the position taken by its counsel as to sentence following a guilty plea. I do not doubt that we have discretion to maintain an appeal taken by the Crown under such circumstances but, in my opinion, we should do so only in exceptional cases, e.g., where there is evidence of bad faith or where counsel for the Crown has been led into error. I do not find this to be such a case.

73. *Regina v. Pretty*, 5 C.C.C. (2d) 332 (P.E.I.S.C., C.C.A. 1971).
The accused pleaded guilty to 2 counts of fraud and was sentenced to fine of $1,000 plus probation for 2 years. The accused applied for leave and appeal from sentence. Due to irregularities in it, the convictions and sentences could not have been allowed to stand in the form in which they were.

By consent of counsel for the appellant and the respondent, the court entered proper convictions on each charge to which the appellant had pleaded guilty and heard counsel on the question of the harshness or excessiveness of the sentence since that was the only real complaint which the accused said he had against the sentence.

Accordingly, argument was heard on the question of what would be a fit sentence to impose on the appellant in the circumstances. This is a case where the convicting court thought that a fit sentence would have been a fine of $1,000 and in default of payment to imprisonment for a term of one year and in addition to comply with the terms of a probation order. Counsel for the accused urged that the court should suspend the passing of sentence pursuant to section 663(1)(a) (formerly section 638(1)(a)) of the Criminal Code, and counsel for the Crown agreed to a suspended sentence. This was the same position taken by counsel before the magistrate. The magistrate even though he erred, obviously gave careful consideration to the question of a fit and proper sentence; and were it not for the illegality of the sentence, the court did not think the circumstances would warrant any interference by it. Eventually, however, it did by imposing one month concurrent on each charge and a fine of $250 on each charge also.

74. *Regina v. Fleury*, 23 C.R.N.S. 164 (Que.C.A. 1971).

The accused pleaded guilty to two charges of conspiring with two other persons to commit armed robbery. The Crown submitted that a minimum sentence of 6 months imprisonment would be in order. Two concurrent sentences of 5 months imprisonment were imposed. The Crown appealed alleging their inadequacy and that the trial judge failed to give proper consideration to the representations of the Crown's counsel. On appeal, Crown counsel asked for much longer sentences.

Separate majority decisions dismissing the appeal were written, as were separate dissenting decisions. Montgomery, J.A., at last in the majority, said that:

> It is not necessary for me to repeat at length what I said in my dissenting opinions in the cases of *Regina v. Mouffe*, 4th November 1971 (unreported), and *Regina v. Kirpatrick*, [1971] Que.C.A. 337. Where after a plea of guilty the Crown recommends a light sentence, I do not suggest that this recommendation is binding on the trial judge. He may quite properly state that he intends to impose a heavy sentence and ask the accused whether he wishes to withdraw his plea of guilty. If, however, he accepts the Crown's recommendations, I am of the opinion

> that it is only in the most exceptional circumstances that a court of appeal would intervene. Apart from the possibility that the accused might wish to withdraw his plea, he might wish to make further evidence in mitigation of sentence.

Rivard, J.A., commented, after referring to what Crown counsel said at trial, that:

> Counsel for the Crown was not attempting to fix maximum sentences here, but was merely requesting a minimum sentence.

Clearly, however, representations by the Crown as well as by the defense cannot in any way bind the trial judge. It is desirable, of course, that the representations made by the Crown before the trial and appeal Courts be the same.

Without commenting upon the opinions which could be expressed on this point, and confining myself solely to the circumstances in the instant case, I would, for the reasons given in the material prepared by the trial Judge, dismiss both appeals.

Likewise, Turgeon, J.A., lamented the Crown's *volte face* and said that:

> The trial Judge clearly was not bound by the representations of counsel, but after he had accepted the suggestion put forward by counsel for the Crown, it is incumbent upon the latter to justify its change of attitude, when launching an appeal intended to obtain a more severe sentence. This the Crown has not succeeded in doing, however, and I agree with the following comments made by the trial Judge in the report submitted by him to us in accordance with the provisions of s.609 of the Criminal Code, R.S.C. 1970, c. C-34:
>
> The trial judge is inclined, particularly when faced with a plea of guilty, to adopt the suggestions put forward by counsel for the Crown, since the latter has received the confidential report of the investigating officer and is as a result familiar with certain information and with certain extenuating circumstances of which the judge may be totally ignorant.
>
> Concurring with my colleagues, therefore, I would dismiss both appeals.

Dissenting Judge Casey, J.A., said upon this issue:

> . . . that the suggestion endorsed (five months) by the trial judge had been made by the defense; not by the Crown. This notwithstanding, I assume for the purpose of argument that appellant's representative had suggested six months and that the trial Judge based himself at least in part on that recommendation.

There may be instances in which an accused pleads guilty because he has been promised a light sentence and in such cases the circumstances might well make it eminently unjust for the Crown to appeal or if it does, to succeed. But this is not our case. Subject to this there is no justification for the proposition that the error of its representative should or does deprive the Crown of its right to correct that error by asking this Court to pass on the fitness of the sentences.

Rinfret, J.A., also dissenting, said that the 5 month sentence was suggested by the defense, not the Crown which suggested a minimum sentence of 6 months, presumably for each offense. After referring to statements in *Kirkpatrick* and *Mouffe*, he added that:

> I do not wish, however, to be taken as seeking to deprive the Department of Justice or the Attorney General of their right to repudiate certain statements made by their counsel, where the circumstances so require, nor do I wish to take away their right to appeal a sentence when, in their wisdom, they deem it their duty to do so.

75. *Regina v. Cusack*, 41 C.C.C. (2d) 289 (N.S.S.C., App.Div. 1978).

The accused pleaded guilty to a charge of theft. Opposing a discharge, the Crown suggested a suspended sentence which the Court effectively acceded to in imposing one day in jail (that being the appearance in court) and probation for a period of 24 months plus restitution. The Crown applied for leave to appeal from that sentence, which, apart from the merits, was opposed by defense counsel on the ground that the Crown should not be allowed to change its position but should be bound by the representations originally made. It was noted that the accused had freely entered a plea of guilty to the offense charged before the matter of sentence came before the court for consideration, without any plea bargaining.

Hart, J.A., for the court, said that the circumstances in which the court should decide whether or not to vary the sentence included the Crown's original representations. On this issue, he said, having decided that the facts of the case called for a heavier sentence, that:

> The only remaining question is whether or not any change should be made in the sentence imposed by the learned Magistrate when the sentencing was carried out with the apparent approval of the Crown counsel appearing at the trial. Although there is no doubt that an appellate Court has the power to vary a sentence imposed with the approval of the Crown officer, there is some division of judicial opinion as to whether such a Court should do so under certain circumstances.

A review of the various decision indicates to me that the only reluctance to change a sentence imposed with the approval of the Crown by appellate Courts is in those situations where there has been an attempt made at plea bargaining. It has been considered unfair to the accused who has entered a plea of guilty on the understanding that the Crown will not oppose a certain sentence to permit the Crown by appeal to repudiate its original position.

Considering several authorities, he said this of the dissenting reasons of Montgomery, J.A., in *Mouffe*:

> He appears to be applying the *Agozzino* result to all representations made by Crown counsel at the time of sentence, and I find myself unable to agree with this extension.

After mentioning *Fleury*, he said:

> In my opinion, it is a different matter for a Court to have representations made as to the sufficiency of sentence by the Crown after a plea of guilty or a conviction after trial than it is for the Crown to take a certain position before the Court in exchange for an undertaking to enter a guilty plea. Even though I do not wish to express any opinion as to the propriety of plea bargaining, if a bargain is reached then it is a different thing for the Crown to change its position upon appeal than it would be if no bargain had been arranged.

It is sometimes very helpful for a trial Judge to have the opinion of Crown counsel as to quantum prior to imposing sentence. The trial Judge, of course, is not bound by such opinion and it is, if given, but one factor to be considered in determining the appropriate sentence. I reiterate, and strongly emphasize, that the trial Judge is in no way bound by the representations of Crown counsel as to the quantum of sentence, nor should the Crown in its appellate capacity always be bound by the view of its counsel at the trial. In my opinion, an appellate Court must be free to consider the representations made by the Crown as one factor only in determining the fitness of sentence except in plea bargaining situations, and even there in exceptional circumstances such as those referred to by Montgomery, J.A., in the *Mouffe* case, the appeal Court may find it necessary to intervene.

Referring to *Roy* (1972), he accepted Huggessen, J.A.'s remarks to the extent they were limited to the plea bargaining situation and do not refer generally to remarks of Crown counsel upon conviction after trial or ordinary guilty plea. He noted that the distinguishing feature of *Wood* was that a guilty plea had been obtained after Crown counsel had told defense counsel he would not seek a jail sentence, rendering an appeal by the Crown unfairly prejudicial.

Thus, considering the actual impact of the Crown's position before the magistrate on sentence as minimal, the appeal was allowed to vary the sentence to 9 months imprisonment.

APPENDIX B

The Ontario Attorney General Mr. Bales sent a memorandum to all Crown attorneys concerning conduct of plea discussions. This memorandum is reproduced below:

Ontario Attorney General
Memorandum: To all Crown Attorneys
June 30, 1972

Principles Applicable to Plea Discussions

The following are the nine principles applicable to plea discussions which I announced at the meeting of your Association in Ottawa last May 25th.

1. The proper administration of justice is the paramount consideration in all plea discussions, and, as with all the duties of the Crown Attorney due regard must be had for the rights of the accused, the protection of the public and the interest of the victim in accepting the plea of guilty to a lesser or included of fence.

2. The Crown Attorney should do nothing to compel a plea of guilty to a lesser number of charges or a lesser or included of fence.

3. The Crown Attorney should indict only on those charges on which he intends to proceed to trial or, in trials in the Provincial Judges' Court, the Crown Attorney should, with leave of the court, withdraw those charges on which he does not intend to proceed to trial.

4. The Crown Attorney should not consent to the acceptance of a plea of guilty to an offence which has not been committed.

5. The Crown Attorney should not consent to the acceptance of a plea of guilty to a charge that cannot be prosecuted because it is barred at law.

6. In all discussions with defence counsel the Crown Attorney must maintain his freedom to do his duty as he sees fit. Nothing should be said or done to fetter the freedom of the Crown Attorney and the defence counsel.

7. The Crown Attorney may state to defence counsel the views he may give if asked by the presiding judge to comment on the matter of sentence. The

Crown Attorney should not agree to a specific sentence. He may draw the attention of the presiding judge to any mitigating or aggravating circumstances that may appear to him to be relevant and may make submissions concerning the appropriate form and range of sentence. However he should take the clear position that the matter of sentence is strictly for the judge and that any statement that is made cannot bind the Attorney General in the exercise of his discretion whether to appeal against a sentence or not. This discretion of mine however will only be exercised in exceptional circumstances.

8. The Crown Attorney always should consider himself as agent of the Attorney General and, as such, responsible for the proper administration of justice.

9. Apart from exceptional circumstances neither the Crown Attorney nor the defence counsel, either alone or together, should discuss with the judge matters bearing on the exercise of the judge's discretion, in the judge's chambers or any place other than in open court. Where attendance in the judge's chambers is dictated by the circumstances, the Crown Attorney should always request that a court reporter be present to take down the full discussion which should form part of the record of the case. All representations to the judge on which he is to base the exercise of his discretion concerning a plea of guilty should be made in open court.

I recognize that these principles are not new but that, by and large, they have been applied by you throughout the province for some time. However in the interests of clarity, certainty and uniformity I felt that it was advisable to enunciate these principles in order to accord to them some measure of formal recognition.

I wish to stress that these principles are simply what the word "principles" implies and are not rules to be applied rigidly or to be considered binding in every situation. However, although you must have a free and unfettered discretion as to how you will apply these principles, you also have a continuing responsibility to conduct all plea discussions in accordance with their spirit.

These principles are intended to be flexible and subject to revision from time to time. In order that I may make informed decisions concerning any need for revision I expect you to take cognizance of the practical effect of these principles and to inform me concerning their application. I expect you to inform me of any difficulties which you may encounter and to recommend to me any changes which you may feel to be desirable. You might discuss the application and impact of these principles at the regional meetings of your Association so that within the next six months I may receive from you some indication of their effect.

Dalton Bales,
Attorney General

APPENDIX C

The Canadian Bar Association Code of Professional Conduct adopted a rule defining the circumstances under which it is proper to advise a client to enter a guilty plea, and cautioning against doing so where the principal purpose is for expediency. This rule is reproduced below:

When acting as an advocate the lawyer must, while treating the tribunal with courtesy and respect, represent his client resolutely, honourably and within the limits of the law.

Commentary

10. Where, following an investigation,

(a) a defense lawyer bona fide concludes and advises his accused client that an acquittal of the offence charged is uncertain or unlikely,

(b) the client is prepared to admit the necessary factual and mental elements,

(c) the lawyer fully advises the client of the implications and possible consequences, and particularly of the detachment of the court, and

(d) the clinet [sic] so instructs him, it is proper for the lawyer to discuss with the prosecutor and for them tentatively to agree on the entry of a plea of "guilty" to the of fence charged or to a lesser or included of fence appropriate to the admissions, and also on a disposition or sentence to be proposed to the court. The public interest must not be or appear to be sacrificed in the pursuit of an apparently expedient means of disposing of doubtful cases, and all pertinent circumstances surrounding any tentative agreements, if proceeded with, must be fully and fairly disclosed in open court. The judge must not be involved in any such discussions or tentative agreements, save to be informed thereof.[1]

NOTES

1. Canadian Bar Association, Chapter VIII, "The Lawyer as Advocate," *The Canadian Bar Association Code of Professional Conduct* (1974).

APPENDIX D

The report of the Canadian Criminology and Corrections Association showed in 1976 strong disapproval of plea bargaining. Portions of this report are reproduced below:

Techniques:

(a)Abolition by administrative fiat

The Law Reform Commissions of Canada and Ontario have argued that plea bargaining may be eliminated without legislation: all that is necessary is that directives be issued by the Attorneys General to their agents.

(b)Judicial Intervention

The Law Reform Commission of Canada has argued that judges should "use their influence to discourage the practice" of plea bargaining.

(c)Legislation

"a legislative pronouncement that plea bargaining in any form is illegal and would invalidate a guilty plea so procured."

(d)Enforcing Ethical Standards Prohibiting Plea Bargaining

The Ontario Law Reform Commission has advocated that standards of professional ethics should be enforced against counsel who violate guidelines established for the elimination of plea bargaining.

(e)Taking Disciplinary Action Against Police Officers Who Engage in Plea Bargaining

The Ontario Law Reform Commission has put forward the following proposal:

> Together with guidelines to the Crown attorneys, instructions should be issued by the proper authorities to police officers. It should be made a matter of misconduct, for which a police officer may be disciplined, to discuss with an accused person or his counsel any arrangement to plead guilty to any of fence on any understanding or undertaking with respect to sentence or what charges will be prosecuted and what charges will not be prosecuted.

> The police officer should be required to make a full and fair disclosure to the Crown attorney of all relevant evidence and all relevant discussions that have taken place concerning the case.

(f)Destroying the Incentive to Bargain
it has been suggested that the belief that plea bargaining
is vital to the maintenance of a steady flow of guilty pleas
is based on a fundamental misapprehension.

(g)Removing Prosecutorial Discretion in Relation to Serious Charges[1]

NOTES

1. Canadian Bar Association, Chapter VIII, "The Lawyer as Advocate," *The Canadian Bar Association Code of Professional Conduct* (1974).

APPENDIX E

The Ontario Ministry of the Attorney General sent another memorandum concerning guilty pleas in 1976 to all Crown attorneys. This memorandum is reproduced below:

Ministry of the Attorney-General
Office of the Director of Crown Attorneys

Memorandum to:	All Crown Attorneys February 26, 1976
From:	W. H. Langdon, Esq., Q.C. Deputy Director of Crown Attorneys
Re:	Plea Discussions

I refer to the memorandum of June 30, 1972, which Mr. Bales, then Attorney General, sent to all the Crown Attorneys.

The present Attorney General has reviewed the nine principles enunciated in Mr. Bales' memorandum and is satisfied that they are viable and generally are being applied conscientiously in accordance with the underlying philosophy which they reflect. However he has asked me to write to you and emphasize the following matters:

1. Expediency in reducing workload is not acceptable as a reason for accepting a plea to a lesser of fence or to a lesser number of fences. Expediency in this sense does not include weaknesses in the Crown's case on the major charge or charges, which may be a valid reason for accepting a plea to a lesser of fence or to a lesser number of fences.

2. You should be careful to comply with the final sentence of principle Number 9 which reads "All representations to the judge on which he is to base the exercise of his discretion concerning a plea of guilty should be made in open court." This simply means that whenever you accept a plea to a lesser of fence or to a lesser number of fences you should state in open court your reasons for

> doing so. The statement need not be lengthy but should be sufficient to satisfy the public in each case that there is nothing sinister or clandestine in the process of plea discussion.[1]

NOTES

1. W. H. Langdon, Esq., Q.C., Deputy Director of Crown Attorneys, to All Crown Attorneys, February 26, 1976.

CITY CASES, MUNICIPAL COURT, 1919-20; DISPOSITION OF CASES CLASSIFIED BY CHARGES

Charge	Plea unknown	Plea of guilty	Plea of not guilty	Plea not guilty changed to guilty	No papers	Nolle prossed	Other disposition	Discharged	Total
The traffic law violation	6	345	161	11	10	25	2	48	608
Disorderly conduct	1	96	126	1	1	7	4	59	295
Suspicious person	1	22	126	5	10	72	3	55	294
Intoxication	–	180	58	8	–	11	1	18	276
Offenses against chastity	–	85	74	10	3	16	1	28	217
Gambling	1	8	23	–	–	4	–	18	54
Offenses against public health	–	9	8	–	1	2	–	3	23
Offenses against public safety	–	14	3	1	1	–	–	1	20
Offenses against property	–	2	9	–	1	3	–	–	15
Miscellaneous	–	16	10	–	–	1	1	2	30
Total	9	777	598	36	27	141	12	232	1,832

Table I also presents evidence of a high rate of guilty pleas. Nearly one-half of all cases had an original plea of guilty entered, while in a handful of cases not guilty pleas were subsequently changed to guilty. Such occurrences led to the conclusion that some sort of dealing was occurring and quite probably, plea bargaining was in fact taking place.

1. Smith and Ehrmann, *The Cleveland Foundation Survey of Criminal Justice in Cleveland, Part II* (1921), 117.

TABLE II.

FINAL DISPOSITION OF FORTY ONE TRIALS IN 1919

No.	Indictment	Judge at first trial	Judge, final disposition	Nature of final disposition
1	Rape	Baer	Pearson	Pleads guilty to assault and battery, workhouse and fine
2	Burglary and larceny	Baer	Baer	Pleads guilty to lesser offense, Ohio State Reformatory
3	Burglary and larceny	Baer	Baer	Pleads guilty to lesser offense, Ohio Penitentiary
4	Carrying concealed weapons	Cull	Cull	Costs
5	Murder first degree	Cull	Cull	Pleads guilty to second degree murder, life sentence
6	Carrying concealed weapons	Cull	Stephenson	Nolled
7	Burglary and larceny	Cull	Cull	"Bench parole"
8	Burglary and larceny (brother of above)	Cull	Cull	"Bench parole"
9	Pocketpicking	Cull	Kennedy	Pleads guilty to petit larceny, 10 days
10	Neglect to support	Cull	–	Continued
11	Violating auto law	Cull	Cull	"Bench parole"

No.	Indictment	Judge at first trial	Judge, final disposition	Nature of final disposition
12	Burglary and larceny	Cull	Cull	"Bench parole"
13	Carrying concealed weapons	Cull	Cull	Decree vacated, original sentence ordered executed
14	Burglary and larceny	Foran	Foran	Pleads guilty to petit larceny, 30 days and fine, suspended sentence
15	Grand larceny	Henderson	Pearson	Nolled
16	Abortion	Jewell	Pearson	Nolled
17	Auto-stealing	Kennedy	Kennedy	Dismissed, want of prosecution
18	Burglary and larceny	Kennedy	Cull	"Bench parole"
19	Grand larceny	Kennedy	Kennedy	Pleads guilty to petit larceny, $50 fine
20	Cutting to wound	Kennedy	Kennedy	Pleads guilty to assault and battery $50 fine
21	Grand larceny	Kennedy	Kennedy	Nolled
22	Robbery	Kramer	Kramer	Pleads guilty to assault and battery, 30 days and fine
23	Rape	Levine	Pearson	Nolled
24	Manslaughter	Phillips	Pearson	Trial, not guilty
25	Shoot to kill	Phillips	Stevens	Nolled
26	Housebreaking and larceny	Phillips	Bernon	Nolled

No.	Indictment	Judge at first trial	Judge, final disposition	Nature of final disposition
27	Housebreaking and larceny	Phillips	Baer	Nolled
28	Receiving stolen property	Powell	Powell	Nolled
29	Grand larceny	Powell	Baer	Trial, not guilty
30	Cutting to wound	Powell	Powell	Pleads guilty to assault and battery, 3 days
31	Cutting to wound	Powell	Phillips	Pleads guilty to assault and battery, 60 days
32	Manslaughter	Stevens	Stevens	"Bench parole"
33	Cutting to wound	Stevens	Stevens	Pleads guilty to assault and battery, 6 months
34	Robbery	Stevens	Stevens	Pleads guilty to assault and battery, 30 days
35	Robbery	Stevens	Stevens	Pleads guilty to assault and battery, 30 days
36	Robbery	Stevens	Stevens	Pleads guilty to assault and battery, 30 days
37	Robbery	Stevens	Stevens	Pleads guilty to assault and battery, 30 days
38	Burglary and larceny	Stevens	Stevens	Pleads guilty to petit larceny, 30 days and costs, suspended sentence, returned as parole violator
40	Pocketpicking	Stevens	Stevens	Pleads guilty to petit larceny, 30 days
41	Arson	Stevens	Powell	Nolled

1. Smith and Ehrmann, *The Cleveland Foundation Survey of Criminal Justice in Cleveland, Part II* (1921), 149.

TABLE III.

COMPARISON OF GROWTH OF POPULATION, NUMBER OF ARRESTS, AND NUMBER OF PROSECUTORS

	Population of Cleveland	Number of arrests in Cleveland	Number of police or municipal court of prosecutors and assistants	Size of clerical force	Payroll of office exclusive of chief	Salary chief prosecutor
1863	58,241	1,687	–	–	–	–
1880	160,146	7,432	1	–	–	–
1890	261,353	9,616	2	–	$ 1,600	$2,300
1900	381,768	19,923	4		5,300	3,000
1910	560,663	7,185	4		12,300	3,500
					15,300	4,000

Smith and Ehrmann, *The Cleveland Foundation Survey of Criminal Justice in Cleveland, Part II* (1921), 333.

TABLE OF CASES

UNITED STATES CASE LAW

Bergman v. Lefkowitz, 569 F.2d 705 (2nd Cir. 1977)
Boykin v. Alabama, 395 U.S. 238 (1969)
Brady v. United States, 397 U.S. 742 (1970)
Brooks v. United States, 708 F.2d 1280 (7th Cir. 1983)
Brown v. Peyton, 435 F.2d 1352 (4th Cir. 1970)
Commonwealth v. Battis, 1 Mass 95 (1804)
Commonwealth v. Evans, 432 Pa. 52, 252 A.2d 689 (1969) (Dissenting Opinion)
Cortez v. United States, 337 F.2d 699 (1964)
Deloach v. State, 77 Miss. 691 (1900)
Elksnis v. Gilligan, 256 F.Supp. 244 (SDNY 1966)
Garrity v. New Jersey, 385 U.S. 493 (1967)
Gideon v. Wainwright, 372 U.S. 335 (1963)
Mabry v. Johnson, 467 U.S. 505 (1984)
Machibroda v. United States, 386 U.S. 487 (1969)
North Carolina v. Alford, 400 U.S. 25 (1970)
North Carolina v. Pearce, 395 U.S. 711 (1969)
People v. McCrory, 41 Cal. 458 (1871)
People v. Picciotti, 151 N.E.2d 191 (1958)
Pope v. State, 56 Fla. 81, 47 So. 487 (1908)
Santobello v. New York, 404 U.S. 257 (1971)
Shelton v. United States, 356 U.S. 26 (1958)
Spevak v. Klein, 385 U.S. 511 (1967)
Swang v. State, 42 Tenn. 212 (1865)
United States v. Ewing, 480 F.2d 1141 (5th Cir 1973)

United States v. Jackson, 390 U.S. 570 (1968)
United States v. Robison, 924 F.2d 612 (6th Cir. 1991)
Wright v. Rindskopf, 43 Wis. 344 (1877)

CANADIAN AND ENGLISH CASE LAW

Adgey v. The Queen (1973), C.C.C. (2d) 1977
Attorney General of Canada v. Roy (1972), 18 C.R.N.S. 89 (Que. Q.B.)
Brosseau v. R. (1934), 3 C.C.C. 129
Guerin v. R. (1933), 55 Que. K.B. 84
Her Majesty the Queen v. Kirkpatrick (1971), Que. C.A., 337
Her Majesty the Queen v. Daniel Charles Talbot (unreported case no. 454/76 of the C.C.A., released Dec. 14, 1976, Houldon, Martin & Blair, J.J.A.)
Perkins E. Pigeau v. The Queen (1976) 35 C.R.N.S. 222 (Que. C.A.)
R. v. Agozzino et al. (1970), 1 C.C.C. 380 (O.C.A.)
Regina v. Arthur (1978), 39 C.C.C. (2d) 158 (D.E.I.S.C., App. Div.)
Regina v. Askov, et al. (1990) 59 C.C.C. 3d 449
R. v. Regionald Bennett (1991) 3 O.R. (3d) 193
R. v. Brown (1972), 8 C.C.C. (2d) 227 (O.C.A.)
Regina v. Clark (1959), 124 C.C.C. 284
Regina v. Cusack (1978), 41 C.C.C. (2d) 289 (N.S.S.C., App. Div.)
R. v. Dawson (1934), 18 Cr. App. R. 111
Regina v. Ferrio & Richards (reported in Crowns Newsletter, April 1979, p. 39, Ont. Co. Ct., April 3, 1979)
Regina v. Fleury (1971), 23 C.R.N.S. 164 (Que. C.A.)
R. v. Golathan (1915), 11 Cr. App. R. 79
Regina v. Greene (1971), 20 C.R.N.S. 238 (Ont. Co. Ct.)
Regina v. Johnston & Tremayne (1970), 4 C.C.C. 64 (O.C.A.)
R. v. Ingleson (1915), 11 K.B. 512 (C.C.A.)
Regina v. Joseph Lapointe (1978), 2 W.C.B. 199 (Jan. 16, 1978, Ont. C.A., Brook, Martin and Lacourciere, J.A.A.)
Regina v. Mouffe (1971), 16 C.R.N.S. 257 (Que. C.A.)
Regina v. Pretty (1971), 5 C.C.C. (2d) 332 (P.E.I.S.C., C.C.A.)
R. v. Roop (1924), 57 N.S.R. 325
Regina v. Roy (1976), 32 C.C.C. (2d) 97 (O.C.A.)
Regina v. Simoneau (1978), 40 C.C.C. (2d) 307
R. v. Swett (1914), 7 W.W.R. 608
R. v. Wood (1975), 26 C.C.C. (2d) 100 (Atla. A.C., App. Div.)
Rex v. Dorothy Clara Soanes (1948), 32 C.A.R. 136 (C.C.A.)

Rex v. Ford (1932), 17 Cr. App. R. 99
Rex v. Hand (1946), 3 D.L.R. 128
Rex v. LeBlanc & Long (1938) 71 C.C.C. 232 (N.B.S.C., App. Div.)
Rex v. Stone (1932), 58 C.C.C. 262 (N.S.S.C.)
Rex v. Taylor (1950), 34 Cr. App. R. 138
Frank Richard Turner (1970), 54 Cr. App. R. 352 (C.C.A.)

BIBLIOGRAPHY

Aford, D. et al. *Some Statistics on the Preliminary Inquiry in Canada.* Toronto: Department of Justice, 1984.

Alschuler, Albert W. "Plea Bargaining and its History." *Law and Society Review* 13 (1979): 211-245.

"The Prosecutor's Role in Plea Bargaining." *University of Chicago Law Review* 36 (Fall 1968): 50-112.

"The Trial Judges Role in Plea Bargaining." *Columbia Law Review* 76 (November 1977): 1059-1154.

American Bar Association. *American Bar AssociationCode of Professional Responsibility and Code of Judicial Conduct.* Chicago: American Bar Association, 1974.

Project on Minimum Standards for Criminal Justice, Standards Relating to Guilty, Pleas of Guilty, 1968.

Arrigo, James P. "*United States v. Robison and the Enforcement of Plea Bargains Across Federal Jurisdictional Lines: To Bind or Not to Bind?*" DePaul Law Review 43 (1994): 909-962.

"At A Glance, Plea Bargaining." *Chitty's Law Journal* 24 (1976): 78-79.

Becker, Jr., Loftus E. "Plea Bargaining and the Supreme Court." *Loyola of Los Angeles Law Review* 21 (April 1988): 757-841.

Beeman, Yvette A. "Accomplice Testimony Under Contingent Plea Agreements." *Cornell Law Review* 72 (1987): 800-826.

Berkman, Harvey. "Court to Take on Sentencing Rules." *The National Law Journal.* 15 January 1996. A21.

Bettman, Alfred. *Prosecution*. Part II in *The Cleveland Foundation Survey of Criminal Justice in Cleveland*. Cleveland: The Cleveland Foundation, 1921.

Bloom, Robert M. "Judicial Integrity: A Call for its Re-emergence in the Adjudication of Criminal Cases." *The Journal of Criminal Law & Criminology* 84 (1993): 462-501.

Blum, Andrew. "Defense of Indigents: Crisis Spurs Lawsuits." *The National Law Journal*. 15 May 1995. A1.

Blumberg, Abraham S. "The Practice of Law as a Confidence Game: Organizational Co-Optation of a Profession." *Law and Society Review* 1 (1967): 15-39.

Bottke, Wilfried. "'Rule of Law' or 'Due Process' as a Common Feature of Criminal Process in Western Democratic Societies." *University of Pittsburgh Law Review* 51 (1990): 419-461.

Boydell, Craig L. and Ingrid A. Connidis, ed. *The Canadian Criminal Justice System*. Toronto: Holt, Rinehart and Winston of Canada, 1982.

Bruce, Andrew A. "Illinois Association for Criminal Justice Completes Crime Survey." *American Bar Association Journal* 15 (1929): 426-428.

Bureau of Justice Statistics. *Felony Case Processing Time*. Washington, D.C.: U.S. Government Printing Office, 1986.

Burger, Warren E. "The State of the Judiciary." *American Bar Association Journal* 56 (October 1970): 929-934.

Canadian Bar Association. Administration of Criminal Justice Section. "Criminal Report." Attorney General's Record RG 4-02. Ontario Archives, Toronto, Ontario, 1956.

Carmen. Interview by Mrs. C.J.N. Kates. October 29, 1979. Oral History Collection. Osgoode Society of Upper Canada. Toronto, Ontario.

Carns, Teresa W. and John Kruse. "A Re-evaluation of Alaska's Plea Bargaining Ban." *Alaska Law Review* 8 (1991): 27-69.

Casper, Jonathan D. *American Criminal Justice: The Defendant's Perspective*. Englewood Cliffs, N.J.: Prentice-Hall, 1972.

"Did You Have a Lawyer When You Went to Court? No, I had a Public Defender." *Yale Review of Law and Social Action* 1 (Spring 1971): 4-9.

Champion, Dean J. "Private Counsels and Public Defenders: A Look at Weak Cases Prior to Records and Leniency of Plea Bargaining." *Journal of Criminal Justice* 17 (1989): 253-263.

Church, Thomas W. and Milton Heumann. *Speedy Disposition: Monetary Incentives and Policy Reform in Criminal Courts*. Albany, N.Y.: State University of New York Press, 1992.

Circular letter to Crown attorney regarding judges and magistrates granting bail after conviction, 1926. *Ministry of Attorney General Series* RG 4-32, 1956.

Cole, George F. *Politics and the Administration of Justice*. Beverly Hills, Calif.: Sage Publications, 1973.

"Comment to the Amended Rule Changes Concerning Judicial Involvement in Plea Agreements." *Pennsylvania Law Weekly*. 15 January 1996. 11.

Committee on the Reform of the Administration of Justice. Proceedings of a meeting held in Toronto, Ontario. October 3, 1956. Attorney General's Record RG-4-02. Ontario Archives. Toronto, Ontario.

Common, W.B. Minutes of a meeting of counsel of the Canadian Bar Association. Chateau Frontenac, Quebec. September 9, 1960. Attorney General's Record RG-4-02. Ontario Archives. Toronto, Ontario.

Corpus Almanac: Canadian Source Book. Don Mills, Ontario: Corpus Information Services, 1985.

Justice Cou. District Court Judge. Interview by author. Toronto, Ontario. June 1989.

Cousineau, D. F. *Setting Standards for Canadian Criminal Courts: The Case of Plea Bargaining*. Barnaby, British Columbia: Simon Fraser University Press, 1977.

"Criminal Statistics in Anglo-Saxon Countries." *Canadian Law Journal* LIII (1917): 368.

Dambrot, Michael. Head Crown Attorney. Interview by author. Tape recording. Toronto, Ontario. March 10, 1987.

Davis, Anthony. "Sentences for Sale: A New Look at Plea Bargaining in England and America." *Criminal Law Review* (1971): 150-161.

Davis, Robert. "Rosco Pound, Felix Frankfurther, and Criminal Justice in Cleveland." *In Brief* (May 1987).

"Defending a Criminal Case." *Special Lectures of the Law Society of Upper Canada, 1969: Panel Discussion -- Problems in Advocacy and Ethics*. Toronto: Richard DeBoo Limited, 1969.

Del Buono, Vincent M., ed. *Criminal Procedure in Canada*. Toronto: Butterworths, 1982.

Department of the Attorney General. Criminal Appeals, February 18, 1957. Attorney General's Record RG-4-02. Ontario Archives. Toronto, Ontario.

Dershowitz, Alan M. *The Best Defense*. New York: Vantage Books, 1983.

Dodd, W. F. "Progress of Preventive Justice." *The Journal of the American Bar Association* 6 (1920): 151.

Drecksel, Paul Calvin. "The Crisis in Indigent Defense." *Arkansas Law Review* 44 (1991): 363-401.

Dripps, Donald A. "At the Borders of the Fourth Amendment: Why a Real Due Process Test Should Replace the Outrageous Government Conduct Defense." *University of Illinois Law Review* 2 (1993): 261-284.

Dyer, Gregory M. "Criminal Defendants' Waiver of the Right to Appeal -- An Unacceptable Condition of a Negotiated Sentence or Plea Bargain." *Notre Dame Law Review* 65 (1990): 649-670.

Easterbrook, Frank H. "Plea Bargaining as Compromise." *Yale Law Journal* 101 (1992): 1969-1978.

Ejzak, William M. "Plea Bargains and Nonprosecution Agreements: What Interests Should be Protected When Prosecutors Renege?" *University of Illinois Law Review* 1991 (1991): 107-136.

Enker, Arnold. "Prospectives on Plea Bargaining." In *Task Force Report: The Courts*. Washington, D.C.: U.S. Government Printing Office, 1967.

Ericson, Richard V. an Patricia M. Baranek. *The Ordering of Justice, A Study of Accused Persons as Dependants in the Criminal Process*. University of Toronto Press, 1982.

Fauteaux Report. Ottawa: Queen's Printer, 1956.

Federal Criminal Code and Rules. "Rule 11(e)(1)(c)."St. Paul, Minn.: West Publishing Company, 1994.

Feeley, Malcolm H. "Plea Bargaining and the Structure of the Criminal Process. *Justice System Journal* 7 (Winter 1982): 338-354.

Ferguson, Gerard A. and Darrell W. Roberts. "Plea Bargaining: Directions for Canadian Reform." *The Canadian Bar Review* 52 (1974): 497-576.

Fleischer, Lawrence. "Thomas E. Dewey and Earl Warren: The Rise of the Twentieth Century Urban Prosecutor." *California Western Law Review* 28 (1991): 1-50.

Friedman, Hyman. Cuyahoga County Public Defender. Interview by author. Tape recording. Cleveland, Ohio. 1987.

Friedman, Lawrence M. "The Devil is not Dead: Exploring the History of Criminal Justice." *Georgia Law Review* 11 (1972): 257-274.

A History of American Law. New York: W. W. Norton & Company, 1984.

American Law: An Introduction. New York: W. W. Norton & Company, 1984.

"Plea Bargaining in Historical Perspective." *Law and Society Review* 7 (1979): 247-259.

Friedman, Steven L. "Pre-Plea Discovery: Guilty Plea and the Likelihood of Conviction at Trial." *University of Pennsylvania Law Review* 119 (January 1971): 527-535.

Galler, Ed, Provincial Crown Attorney. Interview by author. Tape recording. Toronto, Ontario. March 12, 1987.

______. Interview by Author. March 1997.

Gerber, Rudolph J. "Symposium: Violence, Crime and Punishment." *Saint Louis University Public Law Review* 12 (1993): 225-241.

Glendon, Gordon. Comparative Legal Traditions: Text, Materials and Cases on the Civil Law, *Common Law and Socialist Law Traditions*. St. Paul, Minn.: West Publishing Company, 1985.

Glover, S. "Exclusion of Evidence: Exclusion of Illegally Obtained Evidence from the Prosecution's Case-in-Chief Under the Canadian Charter of Rights and Freedoms." *Canadian-American Law Journal* 4 (1988): 57-81.

Goforth, Carol R. "A Jurisprudential Reflection upon the Burger Court's Approach to Procedural Due Process." *Arkansas Law Review* 42 (1989): 837-885.

Goldberg, Michael A. and John Mercer. *The Myth of the North American City: Continentalism Challenged.* Vancouver: University of British Columbia Press, 1986.

Gorman, Frank. Cuyahoga County Common Pleas Court Judge.Interview by author. Tape recording. Cleveland, Ohio. April 8, 1987.

Greene, Theodore S, John D. Wood, and Allan Arcuri. "Plea Bargaining: Fairness and Inadequacy of Representation." *Columbia Human Rights Law Review* 7 (Fall/Winter 1975-76): 495-527.

Griffiths, Curt T, John Klein, and Simon N. Verdun Jones. *Criminal Justice in Canada: An Introductory Text.* Vancouver: Butterworth & Jones, 1980.

Grosman, Brian A. *The Prosecutor: An Inquiry into Exercise of Discretion.* Toronto: University of Toronto Press, 1969.

Gyurci, Julie. "Prosecutorial Discretion to Bring a Substantial Assistance Motion Pursuant to a Plea Agreement: Enforcing a Good Faith Standard." *Minnesota Law Review* 78 (1994): 1253-1282.

Hagan, John and Jeffrey Leon. "The Rehabilitation of Law: A Social-Historical Comparison of Probation in Canada and the United States." *Canadian Journal of Sociology* 5 (1980): 235-251.

Haller, Mark. "Plea Bargaining, The Nineteenth Century Context." *Law and Society Review* 13 (1979): 273-279.

Harris, David A. "The Constitution and Truth Seeking: A New Theory on Expert Services for Indigent Defendants." *The Journal of Criminal Law & Criminology* 83 (1992): 469-525.

Harvie, Robert and Hamar Foster. "Ties That Bind?: The Supreme Court of Canada, American Jurisprudence, and the Revision of Canadian Criminal Law Under the Charter." *Osgoode Hall Law Journal* 28 (1990): 734-735.

Haynie, Stacie L. and Ernest A. Dover. "Prosecutorial Discretion and Press Coverage: The Decision to Try the Case." *American Politics Quarterly* 22 (1994):370-381.

"Helping to Reduce Crime." *The Kingston Whig Standard*, 14 May 1958. Office of the Legislative Assembly, R.G. 49. Press Clippings Service.

Heumann, Milton. *Plea Bargaining: The Experience of Prosecutors, Judges and Defense Attorneys*. Chicago: University of Chicago Press, 1978.

Hoffman, Walter E. "Plea Bargaining and the Role of the Judge." *Federal Rules Decisions* 53 (1971): 499.

Hogarth J. *Sentencing as a Human Process*. Toronto: University of Toronto Press, 1971.

Hogg, Peter W. "Canada's New Charter of Rights." *The American Journal of Comparative Law* 32 (1984): 283-305.

Horwitz, Morton J. *The Transformation of American Law: 1780-1860*. Cambridge, Mass.: Harvard University Press, 1977.

Hughes, Graham. "Agreements for Cooperation in Criminal Cases." *Vanderbilt Law Review* 45 (1991): 1-69.

Hutchison, Paul P. "Canadians and Americans: How They Are Different From One Another." *American Bar Association Journal* 42 (Nov. 1956): 1023-1026.

Informal Opinions of the Professional Ethics Committee. *American Bar Association Journal* 51 (May 1965): 444.

Innes, Michael. Chief Provincial Crown Attorney. Interview by author. Tape recording. Toronto, Ontario. March 12, 1987.

____. Interview by Author. March 1997.

Johnson, Herbert A. *History of Criminal Justice*. Cincinnati: Anderson Publishing Company, 1988.

Kamisar, Yale. "III. Gideon v. Wainwright: A Quarter Century Later." *Pace Law Review* 10 (1990).

Kamisar, Yale, Wayne LaFave and Jerold Israel. *Modern Criminal Procedure*. St. Paul, Minn.: West Publishing Company, 1995.

Kapunscinski, Judith. "Beyond 'Gideon': 25 Years Later, the Right to Counsel is not Always Assured," *The Los Angeles Daily Journal*. 1 April 1988.

Kaplan, Daniel F. "Where Promises End: Prosecutorial Adherence to Sentence Recommendation Commitments in Plea Bargains." *The University of Chicago Law Review* 52 (1985): 751-772.

Kelso, Robert A. Memorandum. Attorney General. June 1956. Attorney General's Record RG 4-32. Ontario Archives. Toronto, Ontario.

Kinsley, Michael. "TRB From Washington: Inadmissible." *The New Republic*, 6 May 1991.

Klein, A. D. "Plea Bargaining." *Criminal Law Quarterly* 14 (1971-72): 289-305.

Krash, Abe and Anthony Lewis. "IV. The History of *Gideon v. Wainwright*." *Pace Law Review* 1 (1990).

Langbein, John H. "Understanding the Short History of Plea Bargaining." *Law and Society Review* 13 (1979): 261-271.

The Law Reform Commission of Ontario. *Report on Administration of Ontario Courts, Part II*. Toronto: Department of Justice, 1973.

LeSage, Paul J. District Court Judge. Interview by author. Toronto, Ontario. March 11, 1987.

Lieff, Abraham Herman. Supreme Court Justice. Interview by Mrs. C.J.N. Kates. March 3, 1978. Oral History Collection. Osgoode Society of Upper Canada. Ontario Archives. Toronto, Ontario.

Lipset, Seymour Martin. *The First New Nation: The United States in Historical and Comparative Perspective*. New York: New York Basic Books, 1963.

"Canada and the United States: The Cultural Dimension." In *Canada and the United States: Enduring Friendship, Persistant Stress*, ed. Charles S. Doran and John S. Siegler. Englewood Cliffs, N.J.: Prentice-Hall, 1985.

Continental Divide: The Values and Institutions of the United States and Canada. New York: Routledge, Chapman and Hall, 1990.

Lipsey, Richard G. "Canada and the United States: The Economic Dimension." In *Canada and the United States: Enduring Friendship, Persistant Stress*, ed. Charles S. Doran and John S. Siegler. Englewood Cliffs, N.J.: Prentice-Hall, 1985.

Lundquist, John A. "Prosecutorial Discretion: Reevaluation of the Prosecutors Unbridled Discretion and its Potential for Abuse." *DePaul Law Review* 21 (Winter 1971): 485-518.

Lynch, David. "The Impropriety of Plea Agreements: A Tale of Two Counties." *Law and Social Inquiry* 19 (1994): 115-133.

McBarnel, Doreen J. Conviction: *Law, the State and the Construction of Justice*. The Macmillan Press Ltd.: London, 1981.

McGarry, J. F., to Kelso, Robert A. Attorney General. June 16, 1956. Ontario Attorney General's File RG 4-32. Ontario Archives. Toronto, Ontario.

Mackay, Frederick George, Judge of the Appellate Division. Oral History Collection, Osgoode Society of Upper Canada. Tape recording. December 14, 1986. Toronto, Ontario.

Manak, James. "Plea Bargaining: The Prosecutor's Perspective." National District Attorney's Association, 1973.

Mank, Branford C. "Broken Promises and Involuntary Confessions: May a State Introduce Incriminating Statements Made by a Defendant as a Result of Promises in a Plea Bargain Agreement if the Defendant Breaches that Agreement?" *Cleveland State Law Review* 36 (1988): 423-440.

Martin, Arthur G. Ontario Court of Appeals. Interview by author. Toronto, Ontario. March 11, 1987.

Ontario Court of Appeals. Interview by Mrs. C.J.N. Kates. Oral History Collection, Osgoode Society of Upper Canada. Tape Recording. November 8, 1983. Toronto, Ontario.

Martin, Berg and Dan Trigoboff. "Experts Split on Legacy of Historic High Court Ruling; *Gideon* Gets 25 Years Amidst Uncertainty for Indigents Defense; Promise or Reality?" *The Los Angeles Daily Journal*. 18 March 1980.

Mather, Lynn M. "Comments on the History of Plea Bargaining." *Law and Society Review* 13 (1979): 281-285.

Plea Bargaining or Trial: The Process of Criminal Case Disposition. Lexington, Mass.: D.C. Heath Company, 1979.

"Some Determinants of the Methods of Case Disposition." *Law and Society Review* 8 (1974): 187-216.

Mellili, Kenneth J. "Prosecutorial Discretion in an Adversary System." *Brigham Young University Law Review* 1992 (1992): 669-704.

Miller, Herbert S, William MacDonald, and James Kramer. *Plea Bargaining in the United States*. Washington, D.C.: United States Government Printing Office, 1978.

Miller, J. Langley and John J. Sloan, III. "A Study of Criminal Justice Discretion." *Journal of Criminal Justice* 22 (1994): 107-123.

Miller, Justin. "The Compromise of Criminal Cases." *Southern California Law Review* 1 (1927): 1-31.

Miller, Larry W. "Right to Counsel: State Courts on the Front-Line." *Annual Survey of American Law.* 1984.

Moley, Raymond. *Politics and Criminal Prosecution.* New York: Minton, Balch, and Company, 1929.

Morton, Frederick L. *Law, Politics and the Judicial Process in Canada.* Calgary: University of Calgary Press, 1992.

Nardulli, Peter F. "Plea Bargaining: An Organizational Perspective." *Journal of Criminal Justice* 6 (Fall 1978): 217-231.

Nunn, Kenneth B. "The Trial as Text: Allegory, Myth and Symbol in the Adversarial Criminal Process -- A Critique of the Role of the Public Defender and a Proposal for Reform." *American Criminal Law Review* 32 (1995): 743-822.

Ohio Rules of Criminal Procedure. "Rule 11, Pleas, Rights Upon Plea." In *Rules Governing the Courts of Ohio.* Cincinnati: Anderson Publishing Company, 1994/95.

Ohlin, Lloyd E. "Surveying Discretion by Criminal Justice Decision Makers." In *Discretion in Criminal Justice: The Tension Between Individualization and Uniformity.* Ed. Lloyd E. Ohlin and Frank J. Remington. Albany, N.Y.: State University of New York Press, 1993.

Ontario Department of Attorney General. "Education in the Correctional Field." Memorandum, June 16, 1959. Attorney General's Record RGH-02. Ontario Archives. Toronto, Ontario.

Ontario Ministry of the Attorney General. *Report of the Attorney General's Advisory Committee on Charge Screening, Disclosure, and Resolution Discussions.* Toronto: Queen's Printer of Ontario, 1993.

Oral History Collection of the Osgoode Society of Upper Canada. Tape recording, December 14, 1986. Ontario Archives, Toronto, Ontario.

Attorney General's Record RG-4-02. Ontario Archives. Toronto, Ontario.

Outline of the Origin, Growth and Function of the Cleveland Association for Criminal Justice. Cleveland: The Cleveland Association for Criminal Justice, 1921.

Ostrow, Eleanor J. "The Case for Preplea Disclosure." *The Yale Law Journal* 90 (1981): 1581-1622.

Paciocco, David M. "The Judicial Repeal of s. 24(2) and the Development of the Canadian Exclusionary Rule." *Criminal Law Quarterly* 32 (1990): 326-365.

Packer, Herbert. *The Limits of the Criminal Sanction.* Stanford, Calif.: Stanford University Press, 1968.

"Two Models of the Criminal Process." *University of Pennsylvania Law Review* 113 (Nov. 1964): 1-68.

Perras, D. W. "Plea Negotiation." *Saskatchewan Law Review* 44 (1979): 143-153.

"A Pioneer Study of Prosecution." *American Bar Association Journal* 8 (1922): 307-310.

Pizzi, William T. "Understanding Prosecutorial Discretion in the United States: The Limits of Comparative Criminal Procedure as an Instrument of Reform." *Ohio State Law Journal* 54 (1993): 1325-1373.

"Plan Fall Legislation to Tighten Measures on Granting Bail." Attorney General's Record RG-4-02. Ontario Archives. Toronto, Ontario.

Popple, A. E. "Accepting a Plea of Guilty." C.R. 1 (1946): 183.

Pound, Rosco. *Introduction to Crime, Courts and Probation*, by Charles Lionel Chote and Marjorie Bell. New York: The Macmillan Company, 1956.

Pound, Rosco and Felix Frankfurter. *Criminal Justice in Cleveland: Reports of the Cleveland Foundation Survey of the Administration of Criminal Justice in Cleveland, Ohio.* Cleveland: The Cleveland Foundation, 1922.

Price, W. H., Attorney General of Ontario. Broadcast over CKNC on crime prevention, December 6, 1932. Attorney General Series RG-4-32. Ontario Archives. Toronto, Ontario.

Quimet Committee Report. Ottawa: Queen's Printer, 1969.

Rebrovich, Karen. "Factors Effecting the Plea Bargaining Process in Erie County: Some Tentative Findings." *Buffalo Law Review* (Fall 1977): 693-711.

Remington, Frank J. "The Decision to Charge, the Decision to Convict on a Plea of Guilty, and the Impact of Sentence Structure of Prosecution Practices." In *Discretion in Criminal Justice*. Ed. Lloyd E. Ohlin and Frank J. Remington. Albany, N.Y.: State University of New York Press, 1993.

Richards, David J. "The Public Defender Defendant: A Model Statutory Approach to Public Defender Malpractice Liability." *Valparaiso University Law Review* 29 (1994): 511-556.

Rose, Donald J. "Prosecutorial Misconduct." *Georgetown Journal of Legal Ethics* 6 (1993): 1067-1095.

Rosenberg, Benjamin E. "Rethinking the Right to Due Process in Connection with Pretrial Identification Procedures: An Analysis and a Proposal." *Kentucky Law Journal* 79 (1990-91): 259-316.

Rosenberg, Marc. Criminal Attorney, Greenspan & Rosenberg and Professor of Law. Interview by author. Tape Recording. Toronto, Ontario. March 11, 1987.

Rosett, Arthur and Donald Cressey. *Justice by Consent: Plea Bargains in the American Courthouse.* Philadelphia: Lippincott & Company, 1976.

Rossman, Alan, Cuyahoga County Public Defender. Interview by author. Tape recording. Cleveland, Ohio. 1987.

Rothman, David J. *Conscience and Convenience: The Asylum and its Alternatives in Progressive America.* Boston: Little, Brown, 1980.

Rovella, David E. "Fake Plea Bargain in Death Case Raises Concerns." *The National Law Journal.* 9 October 1995. A13.

Rubin, Emily. "Ineffective Assistance of Counsel and Guilty Pleas: Toward a Paradigm of Informed Consent." *Virginia Law Review* 80 (1994): 1699-1722.

Sadd, George. Assistant County Prosecutor and Chief of the Appeals Division for Cuyahoga County. Interview by author. Tape recording. Cleveland, Ohio. 1987.

Sadoff, David A. "The Public Defender as Private Offender: A Retreat from Evolving Malpractice Liability Standards for Public Defenders." *American Criminal Law Review* 32 (1995): 883-931.

Schulhofer, Stephen J. "A Wake-up Call from the Plea-Bargaining Trenches." *Law and Social Inquiry* 19 (1994): 135-144.

Scott, Robert E. and William J. Stuntz. "Plea Bargaining as Contract." *Yale Law Review* 101 (1992): 1909-1968.

Sedler, Robert A. "Constitutional Protection of Individual Rights in Canada: The Impact of the New Canadian Charter of Rights and Freedoms." *Notre Dame Law Review* 59 (1984): 1191-1242.

Sentencing Reform Act of 1984 (Title II of the Comprehensive Crime Control Act of 1984). 28 U.S.C. section 991 (1988).

Sims, Edwin W. "Speedy Justice in Criminal Cases." *The Journal of the American Bar Association* 7 (1921): 598-600.

Skolnick, Jerome H. "Social Control in an Adversary System." *Journal of Complex Resolution* 11 (March 1967): 52-70.

Smith, Reginald Heber and Herbert B. Ehrmann. *The Criminal Courts. Part I in The Cleveland Foundation Survey of Criminal Justice in Cleveland.* Cleveland: The Cleveland Foundation, 1921.

Special Lectures of the Law Society of Upper Canada. "Defending a Criminal Case." 1969.

Standen, Jeffrey. "Plea Bargaining in the Shadow of the Guidelines." *California Law Review* 81 (1993): 1471-1538.

Starkweather, David A. "The Retributive Theory of 'Just Deserts' and Victim Participation in Plea Bargaining." *Indiana Law Journal* 67 (1992): 853-878.

Stenning, Philip P. *Appearing for the Crown*. Cowansville, Quebec: Brown Legal Publishing, 1978.

Stringfellow, Eric and Joseph D. Rice. "An Indictment of the System: Cuyahoga Track Record Hints of Overcharging." *Cleveland Plain Dealer*. 30 April 1991, 1-C.

"Symposium." *Canadian Bar Review* 37 (1959): 1-21.

Tarnopolsky, W. "The Historical and Constitutional Context of the Proposed Canadian Charter of Rights and Freedoms." *Law and Contemporary Problems* 44 (1981): 169-193.

"A Thoughtful Examination of Some of the Major Criminal Justice Issues, with Recommendation for Change." In *Struggle for Justice. A Report on Crime and Punishment in America*. New York: Hill & Wang, 1971.

Tremeer's Criminal Code, the e1997 Annotated Ontario: Carswell Publishing, 1997.

"The Unconstitutionality of Plea Bargaining." *Harvard Law Review* 83 (1969-70): 1387-1411.

Van Tassel, David D., ed. *The Encyclopedia of Cleveland History*. Bloomington, Ind.: Indiana University Press, 1987.

Walker, Samuel. "Exploring the Roots of Our Criminal Justice Systems." *Michigan Law Review* 81 (1982-83): 946-952.

Popular Justice, a History of American Criminal Justice. New York: Oxford University Press, 1980.

Taming the System, the Control of Discretion in Criminal Justice, 1950-1990. New York: Oxford University Press, 1993.

Weaver, John C. *Crimes, Constables, and Courts: Order and Transgression in a Canadian City, 1816-1970*. Montreal: McGill-Queen's University Press, 1995.

Welch, Sarah, Provincial Crown Attorney. Interview by author, Tape recording. Toronto, Ontario. March 12, 1987.

_____. Interview by author. March 1997.

Wharton, Francis. *Wharton's Criminal Evidence*. Vol. 22. Rochester, N.Y.: Lawyers Co-operative Publishing Company, 1912.

White, Kenneth E. "*Mabry v. Johnson*: The Supreme Court Sees the Forest Through the Trees, Reverses Plea Bargain Decision." *The American Journal of Trial Advocacy* 8 (1984-85): 266-292.

Winks, Robin. *The Relevance of Canadian History: United States and Imperial Perspective*. Toronto: MacMillian of Canada, 1979.

Wise, Sydney F. *Canada Views the United States: Nineteenth Century Political Attitudes*. Seattle: University of Washington Press, 1967.

Wishingrad, Jay. "Plea Bargaining in Historical Perspective." *Buffalo Law Review* 23 (1974): 499-527.

Woods, J. G. "Criminal Justice History in Canada: A Brief Summary of Work in Progress." *Criminal Justice History and International Annual*. Westport, Conn.: Meckler Publishing, 1984.

Zeno, Thomas E. "A Prosecutor's View of the Sentencing Guidelines." *Federal Probation* (December 1991): 31-37.

INDEX

www.ingramcontent.com/pod-product-compliance
Ingram Content Group UK Ltd.
Pitfield, Milton Keynes, MK11 3LW, UK
UKHW021907150926
475560UK00003B/230

9 780761 811084